MW00624825

THE

GREAT

REBOOT

Succeeding in a World of Catastrophic Risk and Opportunity

BOB ZUKIS
PAUL FERRILLO
CHRIS VELTSOS

DDN Press
www.digitaldirectors.network

Printed in the United States of America
First Printing 2020
First Edition 2020

ISBN: 978-1-7350430-9-8

Library of Congress Control Number: 2020908746

10 9 8 7 6 5 4 3 2 1

The authors make no representations or warranties with respect to the
accuracy or completeness of the contents of this work and specifically
disclaim all warranties, including without limitation warranties of fitness for a
particular purpose. Under no circumstances, shall any of the information
provided herein be construed as legal advice of any kind.

Requests for permission or bulk discounts should be directed to
contact@thegreatreboot.info.

*To those who battled COVID-19 and to the ones who
treated, cared for and comforted them.*

Skye!

You inspire me.

Thans for leading the

way on how to be of

service-

Chris

Acclaim for
THE GREAT REBOOT

THE GREAT REBOOT needs to be read by every CEO and Director to help them make sense out of the strategic and operational risks hitting them head-on from the pandemic to understand how their digital business system will safely and successfully see them through this. Most importantly, CEOs and Directors need to act on systemic risk—before it's too late—again.

-Bob Kress, Accenture Security Group Operating Officer

THE GREAT REBOOT offers a fantastic perspective on the digital ecosystems surrounding the post-COVID economic reset and the enormous changes that companies must respond to. A great read that will reframe the future for any business leader.

-Phil Gardner, Founder & CEO IANS

This book touches on one of the most critical issues all businesses face today. We highly recommend that everyone read and study this book.

-Scott Becker, Publisher Becker's Healthcare, Partner McGuireWoods

Business leaders need a way to safely navigate their way out of the pandemic. This book is a just-in-time roadmap for turning disaster into strength.

-Kate Fazzini, Cybersecurity Reporter CNBC

The simple, accessible, holistic DiRECTOR framework described in THE GREAT REBOOT acts as a springboard to help business leaders to develop and plan their mindset on the new normal with its practical business examples.

-Antonio Rallo, Founder and CEO ID345.TECH
& Co-Founder KioNetworks.com

THE GREAT REBOOT artfully and interestingly discusses the systematic failure of the American system at its root. The COVID-19 pandemic exposes both the magnitude of complexity as well as our leadership failures. Without a complete paradigm shift and reboot, we will end up in the same place with nothing learned from this virus.

-Tony Cioffoletti, Director NY InfraGard

This is an incredibly timely, thought-provoking and practical guide for business and technology executives in our post-pandemic world. It's filled with expert advice on managing systemic risk and—even more critically— understanding how complex digital business ecosystems will impact all our futures.

-Maryfran Johnson, CEO MFJ Media

THE GREAT REBOOT is a powerful message and a wake-up call to all executives in the post-COVID-19 era. Every industry has its own set of issues, but every company's digital operating system is the key to figuring them out.

-Yuka Yeung, Industrial Director EQT, Corporate Director,
Former CEO KFC Hong Kong & Macau

THE GREAT REBOOT gives Boards of Directors and corporate leaders the tools to navigate this digital ocean with sound advice, proven recommendations, and frameworks needed to reach their next destination. We are all charting a new course as the world rapidly evolves. Use THE GREAT REBOOT as your navigator to successfully set sail.

-Brook Colangelo, CIO of Waters Corporation, Board of Directors ISO New England, and Former CIO for The White House during the Obama Administration

This book is for leaders who know that returning to 'normal' after COVID-19 is not an option. It is a guidebook for business leaders who are looking to create new business value post COVID-19.

-Brian Donovan, Executive Coach - Speaker – Author

In times of momentous uncertainty, what separates leaders who will succeed from those who won't is the ability to adapt with resilience. Very relevant reading!

-Duy-Loan Le, Retired TI Senior Fellow and Director Atomera, CREE

At a time when leaders have been completely immersed in adapting to the challenges presented by the pandemic, THE GREAT REBOOT provides a framework to take a step back and broadly assess the risks and opportunities that were brought upon us so quickly.

-Kathryn Hayley, Board Director, Former CEO AON Consulting Worldwide

Table of Contents

INTRODUCTION .... *I*

CHAPTER 1 .... **1**

Flattening the Competitive Curve

   The Driving Forces *6*

   Deep Blue and Bloody Red Oceans *13*

CHAPTER 2 .... **21**

The Chaotic Butterfly

   What's a Complex System? *21*

   Systemic Failure and Small Parts *25*

   When Leaders Don't Understand *30*

   The Complex System is the Next Normal *33*

CHAPTER 3 .... **39**

COVID-19: A Systemic Failure

   Understanding Complex Systems Risk *39*

   Critical Constraints and Total Meltdown *42*

   The Weakest Link Matters Most *45*

   Leadership in Complex Systems *47*

CHAPTER 4 .... **51**

The Complex Digital Business System

   Business Value and Purpose *52*

   The Eight Parts: DiRECTOR™ *53*

   The Key Causes of Systemic Risk *57*

   The Cybersecurity Free-Rider *60*

CHAPTER 5 .... **69**

Complex Systems Enterprise Risk 2.0

   Strengthening ERM 1.0 .... *69*

   What's at Stake and What's the Risk? *72*

CHAPTER 6 .... **77**

Systems Thinking and the Equifax Breach

　Mapping a Complex Digital Business System...............................*77*

　The Equifax Story *79*

　Business Value — What's at Stake................................*80*

　A Technology Debt That Came Due................................*82*

　A Systems Thinkers' Visualization *87*

CHAPTER 7 .... **97**

Cybersecurity — A Unique Risk

　Driving in a Snowstorm..*100*

　The One Cybersecurity Leadership Question................*104*

　Zoom: Systemic Change and New Risk......................*107*

CHAPTER 8 ....**113**

A Deep Blue Ocean Appears

　The RealWear Story..*114*

　The External Forces Driving RealWear..........................*121*

CHAPTER 9 ....**125**

The Post-Pandemic Boardroom

　Governing Complex Systems *125*

　Post-Pandemic Board Development............................*127*

CHAPTER 10...**133**

The Leaders' Post-COVID-19 Roadmap

　Becoming a Systems Thinker and Leader *136*

　How Systems Thinkers Lead.......................................*141*

　Summary *143*

ACKNOWLEDGEMENTS **145**

ENDNOTES **147**

ABOUT THE AUTHORS

BOB ZUKIS

Bob is the CEO and Founder of Digital Directors Network, the world's only organization working to advance the practice and profession of digital and cybersecurity risk oversight in the corporate boardroom. He is an Adjunct Professor of Management and Organization at the USC Marshall School of Business where he teaches corporate governance, strategic management and global business issues.

Bob is a Conference Board ESG Center Fellow and a retired PwC Advisory Partner, a role in which he worked and lived on four continents across twenty countries on the frontlines of globalization. He is the author of the book *Social Inc.*, also of several book chapters on digital and cybersecurity risk oversight and writes regularly in Forbes.

Contact Bob at bob@digitaldirectors.network.

PAUL FERRILLO

P aul is a Partner at McDermott, Will & Emery and focuses his practice on corporate governance issues, complex securities class action, major data breaches and cybersecurity, corporate investigations and work with audit committees and special committees. Paul represents clients across a wide range of industries, including retail, aerospace contractors and sub-contractors, apparel, financial services, investment banking, private equity, hedge funds, 1940 Act funds, energy, oil and gas, and real estate.

He is an Adjunct Professor at the Florida State University School of Law where he teaches cybersecurity law and policy, as well as lecturing on federal securities law at the Harvard University School of Law.

Paul is co-author of the book *Take Back Control of Your Cybersecurity Now*.

Contact Paul at pferrillo@aol.com.

CHRISTOPHE VELTSOS

C hris is a Professor in the Department of Computer Information Science at Minnesota State University, Mankato where he regularly teaches cyber-security courses and oversees a cyber risk graduate program.

Chris also helps leaders and their organizations take stock of their digital risks and manage them across the intricate landscape of technology, business, and people.

Chris is co-author of the book *Take Back Control of Your Cybersecurity Now*.

Contact Chris at chris@drinfosec.com.

Introduction

COVID-19 has stopped the world.

Every business and system on the planet now needs to reboot. The challenge of restarting them is unprecedented.

But so are the opportunities. This book is a story of extraordinary risk and opportunity for business leaders, the story of the largest systemic failure in our lifetimes, and the systemic transformation that must follow.

It teaches business leaders how to be systems thinkers, how to not only restart, but also to reimagine the world they can bring into being with their own digital business systems leading the way.

Not because they can, but because they must. Because the world that we created failed us.

Restarting economies isn't only about reopening businesses exactly as they were; every business also needs to be relevant in a post-pandemic world.

They need to be reopened and reborn into the strategic risks they now face and the new needs and wants they'll now need to serve.

Many businesses were already struggling through a difficult transformation as they were adapting to a digital future. But COVID-19 has now infected every humanmade system on the planet. That compounds their challenge, but also provides the catalyst that they needed. Every one of the systems that we've created now faces a new future. One filled with new possibilities, because the widespread impact of the pandemic has made that unavoidable.

Every company's digital business system remains not only central to its value proposition, but also, it's now the *only* market and employee engagement channel available to many of them.

While CIOs and CISOs have already been at the forefront of keeping businesses connected and functioning during the pandemic, they'll become even more vital in its aftermath.

So, just as computers follow a reboot sequence, a global post-pandemic reboot cycle also has its starting point. It begins with business leaders—forward-thinkers who can see and enable new possibilities behind massive change.

A full reboot from COVID-19's devastation calls for a deep understanding of how a healthcare crisis managed to cascade and infect political, economic, social, and business ecosystems. An unprecedented collection of catastrophes, but they may have a silver lining in their delivery of a necessary wake-up call.

This is a defining moment that creates a once-in-a-generation opportunity to challenge old assumptions

—Pat Gelsinger, CEO VMWare.[1]

The world is full of complex systems, natural ones, and those constructed by humankind. Modern systems increasingly rely on a digital backbone to fulfill their purpose. And almost all businesses are powered by an increasingly complex digital operating system.

But our understanding of how these complex systems work and function is carelessly lacking. We built them because we could, yet we haven't worked nearly hard enough to understand them as well as we need to.

These complicated systems were built without any masterplan, cobbled together as a collection of parts like Frankenstein's monster.

We've now painfully discovered how they can let us down, and we're all experiencing the risk and widespread impact of colossal systems failure.

But within this failure lies the potential and necessity for widespread systemic change.

Systemic risk and failure were the causes of the COVID-19 catastrophe and its far-reaching devastation. They're failures that didn't need to happen. Understanding how small risks evolve to become big failures will prevent them from happening again.

All complex systems comprise many interconnected elements working together to fulfill an intended purpose. This means every business is a sophisticated collection of complementary parts, powered by a critical digital subsystem.

If this digital system shuts down, however, many businesses will grind to a halt exactly as some have experienced with cybersecurity failures—and as countless more have come to appreciate during the COVID-19 crisis.

Business leaders have a newfound understanding for how vital their digital leadership teams and systems are to their existence.

The complex digital systems powering companies are conceptually like the human body's own critical subsystems; here, circulatory, respiratory, immune, nervous, and digestive systems—among others—all work together to enable and sustain life. And we are only just beginning to understand how COVID-19 impacts the complicated system that is the human body.

But we do know that we'll figure it out, just as we need to figure out our other complex systems.

In the humanmade world, we already have the capacity to design highly complex and reliable—although not always infallible—physical systems. What frequently eludes us, however, is understanding how and why larger systems behave the way they do and how different systems interact.

The bigger picture needs to be conceptualized at a different level by leaders possessing the will and ability to bring it into focus to safely reshape a new future.

They need to understand these complex systems' components and how they work together, also recognizing how and why micro-level changes flow and impact the larger system. Leaders must grasp how even the tiniest risk or failure can become a global disaster, taking timely steps to prevent it from becoming a reality.

The fact that the systems we've created have become progressively complex is not necessarily a bad thing; it's rendered them able to serve an increasingly broad and diverse collection of wants and needs for a global population of almost 8 billion.

In fact, they've grown complex precisely *because* of these demanding and varied needs and wants.

But as we're now finding out, their strength can also be their vulnerability, offering up more weak points where risk can enter to threaten and overwhelm the system in catastrophic ways.

Studying complex systems is a relatively new scientific approach. It's also an increasingly necessary one.

In THE GREAT REBOOT, we're introducing these fundamental concepts to business leaders to help them understand the complex digital business systems powering their companies.

It's these vital systems that will enable them to capitalize on the forceful waves of post-pandemic change as they spread far and wide.

These powerful waves of systemic change are already arriving, the potency they bring demands new thinking—new paradigms.

It's illogical to revert the future to a failed past. And massive change can often be easier when it's forced—when there is no choice.

Sometimes, that's the only way it will happen.

Louis Pasteur, the famous systems thinker and micro-biologist said in 1854:

In the fields of observation,
chance favors only the prepared mind.

THE GREAT REBOOT will teach corporate leaders to recognize, understand and apply key systems-thinking principles as an aid to navigating the massive changes and risks this global pandemic has brought onto their businesses.

They'll be able to understand the systemic risks inherent in their own complex digital business systems, then learn to extend this thinking into navigating the systemic changes that will define their company's future.

The world that we've built and the systems within it have failed us.

We have no choice now. It's time for a reboot.

Bob Zukis
Manhattan Beach, California
June 2020

BOB ZUKIS | PAUL FERRILLO | CHRIS VELTSOS

Chapter 1

Flattening the Competitive Curve

For every company, a great equalizing in competitive markets is occurring because of the universal disruption being caused by the pandemic.

That's both the big risk and the big opportunity behind systemic change.

Long-standing markets, consumer preferences, social behaviors, industry disruption, habits, business models, value propositions, and competitive advantages are all changing. These impacts will differ by sector and demographic and can be significant or subtle.

Even digitally native brands will have to challenge their own status quos to adapt to this new normal.

— Katia Beauchamp, CEO Birchbox[2]

Systemic failure incentivizes systemic change as it exposes things that didn't work alongside the realization that entire systems can function much more effectively.

Compounding this challenge are the changes happening behind each system's very purpose. Does that purpose still exist, or has a new want, need and purpose taken its place because of COVID-19—one rendering the point of the old system irrelevant?

The global travel and hospitality industries are already facing survival-level issues. Even the value propositions for technology-led disruptors such as Airbnb and Uber are suffering massive displacement.

Stay-at-home companies like Amazon and Netflix are early beneficiaries, but is their momentum temporary, or permanent?

The restaurant industry contributes approximately 4% to U.S. GDP[3] and estimates are that up to one third of restaurants may close permanently because of the pandemic[4].

The oil industry is suffering massive oversupply and price declines as stay-at-home practices severely reduce fuel consumption.

Weaknesses in healthcare systems have been exposed, but so have some strengths.

Food supply chains are being interrupted, higher education is flailing, the gambling industry has stopped and there are both shortages and excesses in non-durable consumer products.

Car sales have plummeted, there's much less air and vehicle traffic, toll roads are collecting fewer tolls, the skies and our waters have cleared of pollution and automobile insurance companies are giving rebates.

The sporting industry is at a standstill, and personal services have halted. Commercial and residential real estate rents are going unpaid and prime properties are sitting unsold, shared office space is becoming far less attractive—and the list goes on, as the cascading devastation of COVID-19 continues.

These early disruptions are obvious; many won't be.

Existing markets will change, and new ones will appear because of COVID-19.

ISSUE IN ACTION: THE MEAT INDUSTRY

The meat supply chain is being impacted by COVID-19 and this key part of the food production system is starting to show signals of systemic change.

The meat industry is the largest U.S. agriculture segment and back in 2012, it was estimated to contribute US$894 billion to the American economy, or about 6% of U.S. GDP[5].

But, is a new paradigm emerging because of COVID-19?

Beyond Meat (NASDAQ: BYND) is a company that pioneered plant-based meat equivalents, i.e., a plant-derived hamburger, yet tasting, looking and feeling like an animal-derived hamburger. Its value proposition is to offer products that are "…better for you and the planet[6]."

A convergence of both direct and indirect external forces all driven by COVID-19 is expanding Beyond Meat's market and creating disruption to the legacy sector. Compounding this are changes in consumer behavior. Is this a brewing storm of external forces and systemic change?

Here's how events are unfolding:

A virus (COVID-19) originally reported by the Chinese CDC[7] as derived by consumption of an infected animal launched a global pandemic and heightened awareness and concern of meat-based consumption to certain consumer segments. Beyond Meat is popular with millennials as a key demographic. Videos of the Chinese wet markets like the one that reportedly spawned the infected meat were viewed widely, further shaping consumer opinion and perspectives.

As the virus spread into rural America, concentrations of COVID-19 infections started occurring in America's meat processing facilities in early May, leading to meat supply chain shortages, further raising COVID-19-induced distress about the supply, quality and safety of meat-based food production. Wendy's reported that 20% of their fast food restaurants had no beef products by early May[8].

Consumer concerns and awareness continue to spread beyond the company's core millennial demographic as the news of meat supply chain problems become widespread. Is this convergence of external forces driving permanent change in consumer preference, making consumers more open to meat substitutes and alternatives? Will fear, uncertainty and doubt, and a mistrust of meat-derived products permanently drive consumers away, shrinking this market?

COVID-19-driven disruption hits the legacy meat industry from multiple angles through production problems and shutdowns, while the forces of shifting consumer preferences converge to deliver a delicious recipe for systemic change.

It remains to be seen if this initial impact is a short-lived or permanent market shift. We believe it is the start of a permanent systemic shift in consumer tastes away from meat, not just in America but globally, and that large untapped markets for alternative non-animal derived food products will open based on

> changing consumer needs and wants driven by anxiety over the virus' possible source.

The journey for business leaders starts with resuscitating their businesses. But, bringing them back to what kind of life? Their approach needs to comprise more than attempting to return to normal. Their old normal is gone, or at least significantly altered.

The Driving Forces

The very popular 2005 business book *Blue Ocean Strategy* focused business strategists not on head-to-head competitive differentiation, but on making or finding uncontested markets.

As a powerful conceptual model, its concentrated business leaders on redefining value through innovation, opening, capturing and defining a new market space.

The authors referred to these new spaces as "Blue Oceans."

In this way, companies could avoid the traps and competitive intensity of competing on value or price or getting lost in the middle where the company had neither a clear value or price-based proposition and was lost in no-man's land.

In finding these Blue Oceans, the conceptual model emphasized a focus on what customers valued, fulfilling their unmet needs while also redefining the delivery model. In this way, businesses could carve out a unique value proposition with little competition.

Marvel Studios, Apple, Salesforce and Amazon—and a long time ago—Ford, are often cited as companies creating their own Blue Oceans by innovatively fulfilling unmet needs and wants.

Beyond Meat is also finding its ocean getting deeper and bluer as the days pass.

Changing needs and wants present new, often un-serviced requirements. Finding these Blue Oceans requires creative, adaptable leaders playing a game never played before. In this game, they can be the best—perhaps the only one in the world capable of playing it.

The impact of COVID-19 on entire market structures and systems is what capitalizing on systemic change is all about. Vast pandemic-driven shifts create new markets, needs and wants, all catalysts for unprecedented levels of structural change.

The forces of external change driving structural reform are momentous and encompass social, technological, economic, environmental, political, legal, ethical and demographic shifts. Many of these will be tectonic, felt far and wide. Their aftershocks will occur for years.

The acronym for these shifts is STEEPLED, a useful, long-established strategic management method for analyzing external forces of change.

Understanding the compound effects of the scale and scope of these forces is where systems thinkers excel.

The STEEPLED framework is useful both at a macro level and a micro level, the latter delivering subtle but impactful insights.

Systems thinkers know that small events can have big impacts on large systems, and they'll excel at understanding the details.

Systemic change and opportunity starts with understanding and anticipating these many forces of change and the new markets they will create, and the legacy ones they will disrupt.

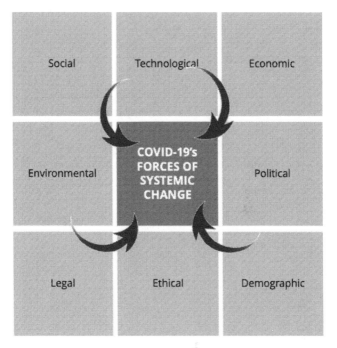

Figure 1—COVID-19's Forces of Systemic Change © DDN LLC

A pre- and post-COVID macro analysis of changes using the STEEPLED framework explains some of the large shifts already taking place across America.

Assessing and understanding these—and many other large and small forces of change—is the starting point for business leaders to identify those powers most impacting the future of their business and markets.

SOCIAL	
Pre-COVID	Post-COVID
A meet-and-greet culture.	Aversion to in-person environments of all sizes.
Laissez-faire attitude to situational hygiene.	Validated cleanliness as a high-priority value driver.
Bulk purchases.	Faster consumption cycles, selective stockpiling.
Online ordering and delivery as a secondary channel.	Online ordering and delivery as the preferred channel.
Work-life balance.	Life-work balance.
High environmental touch interactions.	Low environmental touch interactions.
Casual home offices.	Professional home offices.
Let's go!	Why go?
Co-workers as family.	Family as family.
Blind trust in systems.	Validated trust in systems.
Online ego, vanity and self-fulfillment.	Finding meaning offline.
Consumption-focused.	Savings-motivated.
Healthcare as a nicety.	Healthcare as necessity.
Casual personal relationships.	Careful personal relationships.
Reluctantly active.	Activity means healthcare.
Home as refuge.	Outside as refuge.
Climb the ladder at work.	Hold onto the ladder and look for other ladders.
Mass transportation, open access.	Modular transportation, trusted access.
Long commutes to work.	Ten-foot commutes to work.

TECHNOLOGICAL	
Pre-COVID	Post-COVID
Digital as a business afterthought.	Digital as a core business value driver.
CIO as subject matter expert.	CIO as value creator and business executive.
Aversion to online video.	Video natives and broader expectations.
Uneven adoption, and new technology apathy.	Mass adoption, and an appetite for new technology.
CEO and boardroom as digital transformation and risk observers.	CEO and boardroom as digital transformation and risk champions.
Uneven employee engagement as a part of the cybersecurity system.	New employee responsibility to the cybersecurity system.
CISO as a cost center.	CISO as a value protector.
Robotics as a human productive enhancer.	Robotics as a worker replacement.
ECONOMIC	
Low employment, high consumer confidence and GDP growth.	Massive unemployment, consumer fear and shrinking GDP.
Rise of the global marketplace, price-driven sourcing, and remote threats to large corporates.	Insourcing, reliability focused, rapid capital reallocation to post-pandemic growth sectors.
Shareholder primacy rules.	Other stakeholder power gains.
Global supply chains.	Glo-cal supply chains with more redundancy.

ENVIRONMENTAL	
Pre-COVID	Post-COVID
Corporate greenwashing.	Green as a critical risk and growth driver.
Climate-change denial.	Clear skies, waters and a clear view on humanity's negative impact on the planetary system.
Environment as an isolated system.	Environment as a critical part of every system.
POLITICAL	
Polarization as a strategy.	Leadership as a necessity.
Opinion-based.	Expert-influenced; fact-based.
Receding U.S. Federal government.	Rise of the State, new role of the U.S. Federal government.
LEGAL/ETHICAL/DEMOGRAPHIC	
Sporadic digital regulation.	Far-reaching and universal regulation; digital rights vs surveillance debates.
Cybersecurity fines, after-the-fact board and leadership accountability.	Before-the-fact, digital and cybersecurity risk oversight responsibility.
Companies as short-term employers and at-will employment.	Companies as stewards of long-term employee well-being, development and employment.
Inattention to ageing population, strangling migration and multi-generational me-first priorities.	Care and capitalizing on global and multi-generational talent for innovation and a common purpose.

Deep Blue and Bloody Red Oceans

As these and many more changes take hold, four distinct segments will emerge across most markets.

Large markets where systemic or paradigm-shifting change is high will present companies with new opportunities for growth through innovation and new value propositions; industry boundaries will move as new needs and wants emerge.

These shifts will also introduce disruptive risks to established companies.

Where the impact of systemic change is small, the markets will be shrinking, crowded and gory. Head-to-head competitive intensity will lower prices, as many suppliers fight for survival.

Consumers will win as economic slowdown will compound these issues as competitors battle for a shrinking wallet and customer base.

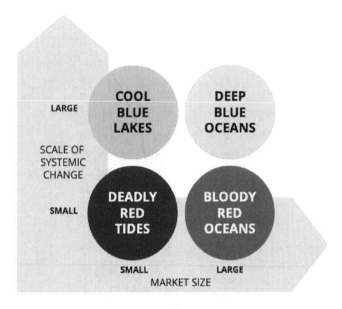

Figure 2—COVID-19 Systemic Change Impact Map © DDN LLC

DEEP BLUE OCEANS — Large markets undergoing structural change will present opportunities for new value propositions with little initial competition. Many new species of companies will be born from these oceans as innovation creates new and exciting consumer-centric offerings to meet shifting post-pandemic demands. These new value propositions will be digitally empowered and delivered by digitally transformed operating systems. These companies will invest heavily in priming their future as the new post-COVID-19 leaders.

14

COOL BLUE LAKES — Creative leaders will look to redefine value propositions wherever they can find opportunity, both upstream and downstream in their sectors, and far afield where systemic change is occurring. Speed will define success and while changes in smaller sectors or sub-sectors may be harder to find, they'll still offer fertile fishing. Systems-thinking leaders will scout beyond their typical industry boundaries to find them.

BLOODY RED OCEANS — Where there's little structural change, the existing competitors will fight over a shrinking market where consumers have won an enormous amount of power. Competition will be ruthless and drag on as suppliers fail, exit or consolidation starts. Vertical integration and horizontal expansion into adjacent markets may help some companies reclaim some market power and begin to redefine their playing field. Any inability or unwillingness to invest in redefining value and delivery methods will prove a heavy anchor in these sectors.

DEADLY RED TIDES — Small markets that don't undergo structural change act brutally on competitors fishing these waters. These markets will be abandoned either willingly or through failure. As the seasons change and competition thins, a smaller supplier group will make it

15

through and a niche will form, later evaporating over time.

In order to navigate these different waters, every company's pre-existing business strategy needs to be rethought in the context of COVID-19's aftermath. Massive market changes are in control and impacting every business.

Capitalizing on opportunity and strategic risk during periods of massive change needs a systems-thinker's mentality, contemplating what could go wrong, but also what needs to go right.

Every company will need to rethink the business game they've been playing and how they've been playing it, all while the game's rules change around them.

While many business leaders have stepped up and been at the forefront of pandemic response, their challenges are just starting. These leaders, including CIOs and CISOs took the lead in guiding employees, customers, and partners through this uncertainty.

The CIO and CISO have played crucial business continuity roles throughout this extraordinary period. At the same time, they've had to deal with an escalating and changing cybersecurity threat landscape as hackers look to exploit the situation.

Their roles will be even more important during the pandemic's aftermath. The corporate board and other C-suite leaders have a newfound appreciation for the vital nature of their contributions to the organization.

All executives are now the first responders to the opportunities and risks arising from widespread systemic change.

Every company's digital business system is the backbone to power their renewal as this remains the core operating system for their future.

Business leaders have seen the irreplaceable value of digitally connecting with their markets, consumers and employees during the pandemic's chaos.

They'll now learn that digital transformation isn't going away.

It's being reborn alongside the systemic changes and opportunities transforming the world.

I hope that we do use it as an opportunity to think critically about how we want the world to be set up.

—Stewart Butterfield, CEO Slack[9]

Some of the many changes that companies will have to deal with are certain and predictable. Regulatory change is already happening and the shifts it imposes are sudden and relatively clear.

Economic change is certain, but specific impacts beyond massive unemployment and slower GDP growth are less predictable, as is the timeline. Behavioral changes are fickle, yet powerful.

Understanding systemic change starts with being able to anticipate the certainty and predictability of the many different change vectors on a company and its markets.

The big-picture changes are on full display, but with complex systems, it's the smaller changes that often have the biggest, long-lasting impacts.

IDEA KEY CONCEPTS

➲ COVID-19 has introduced massive forces of change that are reshaping markets to which every company needs to respond.

➲ Massive change brings large-scale opportunity and risk.

➲ Industries suffering little structural change will become competitively intense.

➲ Sectors in which there's large-scale systemic change will offer game-changing opportunities.

➲ The CIO and CISO are vital to navigating and safely implementing a post-pandemic strategy.

IDEA IN PRACTICE

➲ Oversee at board level a post-pandemic strategic plan focused on mapping markets against systemic change forces.

➲ Develop internal capability to identify systemic change via cross-functional teams, analyzing the external forces of change and their impacts on customers and markets.

➲ Tune the forward-looking parts of the digital operating system to scan for early warning and opportunity signals of change in your markets and beyond.

BOB ZUKIS | PAUL FERRILLO | CHRIS VELTSOS

Chapter 2

A butterfly flaps its wings in Wuhan, China and causes a hurricane in New York City.

Chaos theory and the butterfly effect are terms and concepts many are familiar with, embodying the observation that small changes or events can have significant impacts on complex systems.

What's a Complex System?

Complex systems, such as the global financial system, are difficult to understand. While system components may be understood, comprehending how they interconnect, relate and react to each other is difficult.

This was apparent during the Great Recession of 2008, when a systemic failure starting in one part of the financial system cascaded out of control.

The basic systems-thinking concepts are straight-forward.

Complex systems comprise three things:

1. Parts;

2. Connections between parts;

3. The system's purpose or function.

Things get difficult when the system has hundreds, or thousands, of parts and when it's unclear how those parts interrelate.

This is further compounded when the system has multiple purposes, or one changing purpose. Comprehending these complexities and acting to address the issues uncovered by systems thinking is far more difficult; this is where failure frequently occurs, just as it did with COVID-19.

Complex systems science is an evolving inter-disciplinary field of study trying to make sense of complex worlds, both the ones we've created and the natural one we occupy. Its concepts and principles have been studied and applied to a wide range of issues and disciplines such as planetary health, social behavior, human health, financial systems, urban complexity, artificial intelligence, and big data.

Our focus in THE GREAT REBOOT is to apply these concepts to the complex digital business systems that are the key to driving the post-pandemic reboot.

This application will help leaders understand the key digital system risks that will power and enable their ability to respond to systemic change, while at the same time helping them to understand how to think about structural opportunity driven by systemic disruption and transformation.

Becoming a systems thinker requires business leaders to apply these new patterns of thinking to the companies they run and the risks they face.

Complex systems are all around us. An automobile is a complex system, as is the planet, the human body, politics, healthcare, and even your family. Businesses too, are all complex systems.

The elements of a complex system operate together to enable an intended function or purpose. But while individual components can often be simple, they become complex in their interactions, dependencies and effects when interrelating.

Complex systems have several key properties making them particularly unique:

- Complex systems can be mechanical, physical, natural, human or may encompass combinations of each characteristic.
- Small events can have large impacts on complex systems.

- Complex systems' behavior is frequently non-linear.
- Complex systems' behavior can be unpredictable.
- Certain system traits may only emerge by understanding how elements interact and behave together.
- Complex systems can spontaneously- and self-organize.
- Some complex systems can change and learn to adapt.

Systems become complex for different reasons. Size, in addition to how interconnected the system's elements are, can render a digital system complex. The disparity of the various digital system elements can layer on levels of complexity. And many digital business systems have different jurisdictions imposing rules on the system, compounding both their complexity and risk within the system.

These issues conspire to make digital business systems complex and difficult to understand and control, exactly why systemic risk runs rampant in most companies' digital environments.

This creates threats that jeopardize entire business systems, which can lead to business failure.

Every person on the planet is now experiencing what systemic failure is like. But we've seen it before.

Systemic Failure and Small Parts

A fundamental rule of complex systems is that small events or risks embedded within their individual elements can sometimes have a significant impact on the larger system.

Enterprise risk management often discounts or ignores small probability risks. Systems thinkers can't.

The space shuttle Challenger disaster in 1986 is an example of this, the entire catastrophic event was triggered by the failure of a small "O-ring" in the Challenger's thrust system.

This simple part failed in the cold, when the launch temperature was just thirty-six degrees Fahrenheit, fifteen degrees colder than any other previous launch temperature.

This component risk and its failure then cascaded, setting off a complete systems failure.

In the disaster's root cause analysis, it's commented that:

There was a fundamental design flaw in the joint that engineers had grown accustomed to and had learned to live with[10].

The Rogers Commission examining the disaster made nine recommendations for the restructuring and redesign of the Space Shuttle Program.

Comprehensive understanding unfortunately came far too late to prevent the failure. But it led to significant improvements in the safety and reliability of the complex Space Shuttle system.

This explains why business leaders need to be systems thinkers, to stop small risks from becoming catastrophic. The Challenger disaster cost seven astronauts' lives and—according to the LA Times—cost the nation US$3.2 billion in 1986[11].

And like COVID-19, the risk posed by this part to the entire system was understood and identified before the disaster.

How a component impacts the entire system is a critical part of systems thinking. These causes and effects are not always linear across the complex system, e.g., if A happens, then B occurs.

The O-ring failure created a cascading effect across multiple Challenger subsystems that caused total system failure. These types of critical failure points are common in complex systems.

ISSUE IN ACTION: AUTOMOBILES

Complex subsystems often exist within larger systems such as the electrical or engine cooling systems of combustion vehicles. A tire is an example of a single element within the automobile's complex system. A flat tire causes the entire vehicle system to come to a stop, making it fail in its intended purpose. While that failure is often not catastrophic, it can be if it happens in the wrong driving conditions.

Spare tires are an easy fix to this systems threat. Run-flat tires are an even better innovation, allowing the vehicle to continue to function at a sub-optimal level, avoiding a systems shutdown. Systems engineers figured out that a flat tire was a critical systemic risk to the automobile a long time ago and designed ways to control this risk.

Ransomware is a systemic danger to entire business systems. Holding data hostage can and has stopped businesses from functioning.

In 2016, the FBI warned that ransomware had become one of the fastest-growing malware threats. And according to Europol[12], the size and sophistication of ransomware attacks is growing rapidly.

Ransomware works because it literally holds a business or organization hostage by preventing it from functioning. This cyber risk looks to enter the network at any point of vulnerability, then acts to quickly spread into other systems eventually reaching core systems with direct access to sensitive and mission-critical business data. The rapid evolution of networked operating technology will only make this problem worse and raise the stakes for what's at risk.

The key issue with ransomware has less to do with the cost of the ransom itself, averaging around $84,000 in 2019[13], and everything to do with the cost of downtime, and in the direst of cases, businesses having to close their doors.

A 2019 survey indicated that 15% of companies suffering ransomware attacks paid up[14], up from 4% in 2018. From 2018 to 2019, the number of downtime days due to ransomware rose from 6.2 days to 16.2[15].

This systemic risk perfectly deploys the hacker's complex systems playbook. It can start small yet hold the entire business hostage leveraging the complex system itself to exert a disproportionate amount of force and risk onto the whole business.

Will other external post-pandemic forces, such as consumer behavior changes, now threaten entire business systems and models?

ISSUE IN ACTION: AIRBNB

Could a new obsession for trusted and hygienic environments destroy the Airbnb business model? Will people be less likely to offer or book this type of accommodation if they have hyper-sensitive concerns about cleanliness or disease transmission?

Will different cultures or demographics behave the same? Is this a temporary or permanent consumer behavior shift? Will Airbnb's market collapse on both the supply and demand sides?

Airbnb has already reacted by implementing a new "Enhanced Cleaning Initiative" for their hosts, to try to address this systemic risk to their entire business model[16].

These pandemic-generated forces pose new strategic risks that may greatly impact many business systems. Figuring them out requires systems thinking.

When Leaders Don't Understand

COVID-19 was a virus first infecting one individual in Wuhan, China, yet it spread to cripple healthcare systems worldwide. This failure then cascaded into many other complex systems around the world, from business to social systems, causing widespread degradation, disruption and failure.

Many political leaders didn't understand the complex healthcare system, the risks within it or how to control them. So, they deployed the most draconian measure possible once the system started to fail. Their only option was to turn off the critical risk associated with the part of the system that was spreading the infection. They shut down the people.

Those who did this quickly and decisively muted the degradation in their healthcare system and the virus's cascading effect across multiple systems. But they still didn't escape the pandemic's negative impacts across these other varied systems.

While these actions slowed the spread of the biological virus and saved healthcare systems from collapsing, it lit the fuse on an "infection" that would infiltrate many other systems. This action created economic infection—contagion that spread into business, financial, and social systems.

When leaders don't understand the risk within complex systems, they have two options when the system starts spiraling out of control:

1. Ignore it, and live with the consequences;

2. Shut down the system and react to the consequences.

Most countries chose the second option, although Sweden chose the first. America chose both. The Federal government selected the first path, and then some of America's states stepped in and chose the second.

ISSUE IN ACTION: PG&E

In 2019, PG&E in California shut down part of their electrical grid in response to high winds and the risk of wildfires, eliminating a systemic risk to their business that was not only difficult to control, but also one that they didn't understand in terms of its impact. Shutting down the electrical system eliminated the risk *and* its unknown impacts.

PG&E weighed the short-term impact of a relatively certain amount of lost revenue against uncertain liabilities related to an out-of-control systemic risk with its far-reaching impacts. They would settle previous claims from wildlife insurers for $11 billion

---

in 2019, due to the fires caused by their infrastructure[17].

Shutting down systems to stop out-of-control risk is a solution of last resort. It's not a long-term one or even an effective short-term choice when the compound effects aren't well understood. And with the complex natural systems that inhabit the world, this option isn't available.

This means we have little choice but to understand the complex systems we've created and the natural ones occupying the world much, much better.

We must apply the same sense of urgency to other pressing but less apparent threats, such as climate change.

—*Paul Hudson, CEO Sanofi[18]*

Fortunately, with our humanmade systems, we cannot only understand them better, we can also *make* them better. And we can be proactive in mitigating their systemic risks and their disastrous impacts in failure.

The Complex System is the Next Normal

For companies to survive and capitalize on the massive, pandemic-incurred changes impacting their markets directly and indirectly, they need business leaders who understand complex systems.

Systemic risk can be managed and mitigated in complex systems, but it first needs to be recognized and understood. Fortunately, this isn't an entirely new concept. Some industries and disciplines have a well-developed approach and an understanding of systemic risk within complex systems.

Systems engineers are highly trained to design and build complex systems, deeply embedding systems thinking in their work.

High-reliability sectors such as aerospace and nuclear energy have long had a high degree of awareness and understanding of the systemic risk and cost of catastrophic failure within these complex systems.

Despite this, failure can still occur, e.g., the Challenger Space Shuttle and the Fukushima Daiichi nuclear power plant disasters.

Analysis of the Fukushima incident indicates that it could have been prevented with a better understanding and application of leading systemic risk practices[19].

The Fukushima Daiichi nuclear power plant disaster, like COVID-19, was a consequence of failing to control risks that were well known and understood.

The analysis of its failure concluded:

The Fukushima accident was, however, preventable. Had the plant's owner, Tokyo Electric Power Company (TEPCO), and Japan's regulator, the Nuclear and Industrial Safety Agency (NISA), followed international best practices and standards, it is conceivable that they would have predicted the possibility of the plant being struck by a massive tsunami. The plant would have withstood the tsunami had its design previously been upgraded in accordance with state-of-the-art safety approaches[20.]

Biologists are also trained as systems thinkers, and the concepts of systems thinking are often applied in organizational design, supply chain analysis and software design.

Systems thinking and complex systems science are not new concepts but applying their principles to strategic change and risk driven by complex digital business systems, is. But business leaders at least know there's a starting point they can build upon, using it to develop new ways of thinking to navigate the complex world.

Over the last several years, many business leaders around the world began to realize that the operating system enabling their business was a digital one. Before COVID-19, some of these companies were in the process of rebooting their businesses through various digital transformation initiatives.

But this level of systemic change was failing on many fronts. Many leaders were struggling with how to both envision and enable their digital futures, and boardroom leadership on digital strategy and risk was the exception, not the rule.

These provincial efforts were going on while companies were also trying to keep their businesses secure in an escalating global cybersecurity war. Failures were frequent and expensive, on both fronts.

Digital transformation initiatives are exercises in massive systemic change, paradigm shifts in how businesses function and how they create and capture value.

Now, every business leader has a new appreciation for how vital their digital business system is to the sustainability and success of their business. Thriving in the post-pandemic world is another massive systemic change exercise.

But these two unprecedented challenges need each other.

It's not hard to envision a far more effective digital world. For many companies, it's easy to envision a far more impactful and secure use of modern digital technologies.

Understanding how complex digital systems drive business value for all stakeholders is the enabling force for paradigm-shifting, post-pandemic change.

Though we will return to normal, it won't be the normal we left behind.

—Steve Huffman, CEO Reddit[21]

Business leaders need to start with their own complex digital business system, which is their bridge to understanding and enabling larger levels of pandemic-driven systemic change.

The promise of the digital future has so far exceeded our grasp, although its risks are already here.

COVID-19 is the catalyst that the digital future needs, and an opportunity to which leaders have no choice but to respond.

IDEA KEY CONCEPTS

⊃   Complex systems comprise multiple parts and connections between these parts, working together to serve an intended purpose.

⊃   They behave in unique ways and the scale of many complex systems makes them difficult to understand and control.

⊃   Every business is a complex digital business system.

⊃   Small failures can have large impacts on complex systems and shutting down the system is not an effective approach to managing risk.

IDEA IN PRACTICE

⊃   Train the board and C-suite to develop systems-thinking competencies.

⊃   Conduct a systemic risk analysis of your digital business system to understand how its parts work together to align with the business value that the system drives and supports.

Chapter 3

COVID-19 has brought the direst of consequences for many people, while billions more have been impacted across multiple levels.

A catastrophic systems failure has been unfolding in plain sight.

What went wrong? Was it possible to understand the risks of this global pandemic and how it could threaten healthcare systems and beyond? Could these threats have been controlled, or stopped altogether?

Moving on from this disaster requires an understanding of the risks and failures causing these entire systems' collapse. To reboot from their impacts, leaders must understand the failures as systems thinkers.

Understanding Complex Systems Risk

Understanding systemic risks means knowing how a risk in one part of a system can spread to threaten the whole.

The systemic risks inherent in a local or global pandemic have been very well understood. As were the actions that would mitigate these dangers and prevent the epidemic from turning into a wide-spread disaster. While that doesn't explain why the catastrophe happened, it is good news in that it tells us we can understand these kinds of difficult issues and their hazards.

In 2017, the World Bank published *Disease Control Priorities*[22]. They dedicated Chapter 17 of the book to the risks, impacts, and mitigations of pandemics.

From an impact perspective, their work identified the following:

-Pandemics can cause economic damage through multiple channels, including short-term fiscal shocks and longer-term negative shocks to economic growth;

-Individual behavioral changes, such as fear-induced aversion to workplaces and other public gathering places, are a primary cause of negative shocks to economic growth during pandemics;

-Some pandemic mitigation measures can cause significant social and economic disruption;

-In countries with weak institutions and legacies of political instability, pandemics can increase political stresses and tensions. In these contexts, outbreak response measures such as quarantines have sparked violence and tension between states and citizens.

The World Bank also offered advice on the steps and activities that could control the potential and its significant risks:

-Strengthen core public healthcare infrastructure;

-Increase situational awareness;

-Once started, a coordinated response focusing on situational awareness, public health messaging, reduction of transmission, and care for and treatment for the ill;

-Surge capacity.

The World Bank's analysis specifically called out the pandemic's potential risks to social, political and economic systems, well beyond healthcare. In hindsight, their assessment mirrored the reality of COVID-19 and its far-reaching spread.

Systems thinkers understand each element in a complex system and how they work together. A key part of understanding complex systems is to understand constraints or risks in one system part and how they can affect the overall system.

In the World Bank analysis, surge capacity is called out as a key issue to mitigating the risks of a pandemic. Surge capacity is vital during a pandemic as it alleviates a constraint on the healthcare system that can cause the entire system to fail.

Critical Constraints and Total Meltdown

COVID-19 exposed several critical constraints within the American healthcare system; these introduced catastrophic risk to the healthcare system that eventually caused risk to spread far beyond healthcare.

According to 2020 survey data from the American Hospital Association (the findings of which relate to 2018), the United States at that time had around 98,000 ICU beds[23] of which almost 27,000 were neonatal and pediatric. And according to their 2019 data, the U.S. also had around 924,000 staffed beds in community hospitals.

The numbers of ICU beds and total staffed beds are critical constraints in the overall healthcare system. There are no substitutes for these, and it's difficult to increase this capacity in a short timeframe.

This makes ICU beds an irreplaceable and critical part in the overall system. The same can be said of the 924,000 staffed beds in U.S. community hospitals.

As U.S. COVID-19 infection rates exploded, the volume of patients threatened to overwhelm this part of the healthcare system. Reported cases escalated from ninety-eight to 802,583 during the forty-eight days from

42

March 4th, 2020 to April 21st, at a compound daily growth rate of 20.65%[24]. At that rate, by May 4th almost 7.6 million people would be infected. The entire country would be infected at that pace by May 24th, only twenty days later.

On April 21st, the reported U.S. death rate from COVID-19 was at 5.5% according to the Center for Disease Control website (www.cdc.gov). If the spread had been left unchecked and with that projected death rate, the American death toll by May 4th projected out to be 418,000 people.

That's over four times the critical systems constraint of 98,000 ICU beds. The systems constraint of 924,000 staffed beds would also have been overwhelmed with 7.6 million infected people.

People would have been dying in their homes. Hospitals would have become anarchic and hospital staff would have fallen victim en masse. The healthcare system would have collapsed, then failed entirely. The end result? No healthcare at all.

But death would have continued, escalating in its impact. Stay-at-home work? People would have stopped working altogether. Widespread disorder and a total breakdown of every aspect of society could have occurred.

There was no other way to model the outlook early in the pandemic's spread, given how little was known about the virus at the time. That's the story the data told at that point.

The American healthcare system had several critical finite constraints in its ability to provide care, while the virus had a rapid and almost infinite capacity to infect, sicken and kill.

And those aren't the only critical constraints in the U.S. healthcare system.

According to OECD data from The Commonwealth Fund[25], the U.S. had 2.6 practicing physicians per 1,000 people in 2018, the lowest amongst the ten reported high-income countries where the average is 3.5 physicians per 1,000.

The patient is also a critical input of the healthcare system for a systems thinker. With OECD data also reporting that the U.S. has the highest rates of obesity, highest chronic disease burden, lowest life expectancies, and the highest rate of avoidable deaths.

And as we also saw, other issues such as enough quantities of Personal Protective Equipment (PPE), ventilators and testing capacity also compounded the threat of a massive healthcare systems failure. There were—and remain—multiple critical flaws in the American healthcare system's ability to deal with a pandemic.

When complex systems are spiraling out of control and their risks aren't understood, there are two ways to deal with those risks as previously mentioned. They can be ignored, or "lived with", which means accepting the consequences. Or, the system can be shut down to stop the risks.

America lacked a unified approach and did both.

A fragile healthcare system with multiple points of systemic weakness was staring down a fast-spreading and lethal disease attacking a highly susceptible, unfit population of over 330,000,000 Americans.

America had the worst global COVID-19 outcome for a reason—a systemically weak healthcare system. With COVID-19, the perfect storm of a global pandemic met the American healthcare system's inherent systemic weaknesses.

The Weakest Link Matters Most

The thing about systems failure is that it's not an indictment of every part of the system. Parts of the American healthcare system are very high performing. America's healthcare workers are stepping up in exemplary fashion and the U.S. system's research arm frequently stands out.

The issue in complex systems, however, is how the entire system functions to deliver its intended purpose. A critical weakness in one part of the system which threatens the entire system can create systemic risk, making the entire system as brittle as that singular point of weakness.

Given what looked like a healthcare system melt-down, the only logical option for some of America's leaders was to take action and shut off the contamination to slow the rate of infection or "flatten the curve" through isolation, then deal with the residual impacts. And, of course, to do it in a short amount of time.

The tradeoff was to do nothing and take our chances and run the risk of the entire healthcare system collapsing, with the potential consequences of that apocalyptic scenario. This passive approach relies on hoping that the consequences wouldn't be too bad.

For business leaders and how they oversee and manage their complex business systems and risk, hoping for the best is never a successful strategy and not what's expected. Business leaders are expected by their stakeholders to be active leaders.

But active isolation has also had significant compound effects that are continuing to spread into every other major system in America. The American consumer's lockdown infected them all.

However, largely because of isolation, the daily rate of infection has declined rapidly. It slowed to a daily growth rate of 3.4% on April 21st, bringing much-needed relief to the structurally weak American healthcare system.

And at least temporarily, it took the risk of the apocalyptic scenario off the table. But the battle is far from over.

Leadership in Complex Systems

Leadership and the human component are critical parts of complex systems.

Bill and Melinda Gates wrote the foreword to the World Bank book in 2017, and Lawrence Summers wrote the introduction. The catastrophic impacts of a global pandemic were well understood, including by some influential leaders.

In 2005, U.S. President George W. Bush said:

Our country has been given fair warning of this danger [a pandemic] to our homeland—and time to prepare. It's my responsibility as President to take measures now to protect the American people from the possibility that human-to-human transmission may occur.

...if we wait for a pandemic to appear, it will be too late to prepare. And one day, many lives could be needlessly lost because we failed to act today[26].

Many more examples show a high level of understanding of the systemic risk and impacts of a global pandemic. But despite this, COVID-19 still seemingly caught many off guard. Some countries, including the United States, much more so than others.

The inevitable analysis of how this happened will uncover many failures and shortcomings. And the role of leadership leading up to and during the crisis will undoubtedly be a central theme.

Regardless of whether the governing body is within a political or business system, effective risk management requires effective leadership. It's a critical part and constraint of any complex system.

This means that understanding the complex risks inherent in any business demands CEO and boardroom leadership.

This is the most critical lesson from COVID-19 for CEOs and corporate directors. Their active leadership is a prerequisite in understanding the systemic risks inherent within their business ecosystem, as is making sure that something is done about it. Many of the catastrophic systemic failures highlighted in THE GREAT REBOOT, failed because of a lack of leadership understanding and action.

Other pressures are also coming to bear on corporate leadership that will drive greater responsibility and accountability to these ruinous risks. The courts in America are increasingly looking for documentation to demonstrate the board's responsible oversight of cybersecurity risk.

Regulators see cybersecurity risk and data privacy as significant public interest issues. Demonstrating and documenting a thoughtful and diligent approach to these issues reduces stakeholder risk and liability.

Shareholders will also demand accountability from corporate directors and CEOs, ensuring they're effectively navigating the post-pandemic strategic opportunities.

Both value creation and preservation are at stake, requiring high levels of business leadership and systems-thinking competency.

COVID-19 is a wake-up call to leaders everywhere.

Its lesson is that while it is possible to understand the risks in complex systems, acting upon them is even more vital.

IDEA KEY CONCEPTS

⮞ COVID-19 was caused by systemic risk and failure that spread into every humanmade system.

⮞ We've proven we can understand the risks in complex systems, both natural and humanmade.

⮞ Many parts of a complex system can be strong, but any system is only as strong as its weakest critical link.

⮞ Leadership is a critical part of a complex system.

IDEA IN PRACTICE

⮞ Financial stakeholders such as institutional investors, credit ratings agencies, shareholders, and governance ratings firms should actively understand and assess corporate systemic risk.

⮞ The board and C-suite should actively monitor and understand how regulators and the courts are changing their views on digital and cybersecurity oversight and where new accountability standards are emerging.

⮞ Systemic risk should be an active boardroom discussion and agenda item.

Chapter 4

The Complex Digital Business System

Pre-pandemic, the World Economic Forum estimated that 60% of global GDP would be digitized by 2022 and that 70% of new value created in the next decade would be based on digitally enabled platforms. They also noted that only half of the world's population currently participated in the digital economy[27].

According to International Data Corporation (IDC)—a premier global provider of market intelligence and analysis in information technology—by 2023, some 52% of global GDP will be driven by digital-transformed enterprises and that by 2024, 51% of IT budgets will be for digital innovation and transformation[28].

Rebooting the world will drive these estimates forward faster than they'd have otherwise advanced for one simple reason. The business of business has always been about innovation. And where there's change, there's innovation, and the tools of innovation are digital.

Digital acceleration is the operating system driving transformative change. Data from April 2020 indicates that 61% of IT leaders surveyed will be accelerating their digital transformation initiatives and projects throughout the pandemic, despite a general slowdown in overall IT spending[29].

The need for business value creation and growth is colliding with the new wants and needs of a global population. As the competitive playing field shifts, digital business systems will be the engines to reboot and renew them.

This makes the complex digital business the starting point for business leaders to become better systems thinkers. By recognizing and understanding their digital business system as a complex one, they'll understand both the risks within it, as well as how it will help them address the systemic changes coming their way.

Business Value and Purpose

Like any complex system, digital business systems are comprised of disparate interconnected elements working together to enable a function or purpose. In the case of every business, that function is the company's strategy, and the objective to create stakeholder value.

Stakeholders include shareholders, employees, customers, suppliers, and the communities within which every company operates. Stakeholders can have competing interests, a key consideration for systems thinkers.

Shareholders are the dominant stakeholder in for-profit companies. They value revenue growth, profitability, capital efficiency, and the positive impacts that these outcomes have on total shareholder returns, i.e., share price and dividends.

But the digital business system that every company operates serves many stakeholder interests. Employees may value and need connectivity, job security, benefits, flexibility, and wage growth. Customers want quality, choice, convenience, immediacy, low prices, and excellent service. These motivations and value drivers and how they're enabled are already starting to shift.

Different stakeholders have different needs, and the corporate board's role is central to balancing them. Corporate directors are already applying a basic level of systems thinking in considering these competing, but interdependent objectives.

The Eight Parts: DiRECTOR™

The DiRECTOR™ framework aligns the eight key domains or elements of a complex digital business system with the value that every company's stakeholders demand, and that the system safely delivers.

These eight parts, or domains, are interdependent and influence the functioning and health of any digital system as well as how it supports and protects business value. The business value produced by the digital system, and the risk to that value can be viewed as two sides of the same coin in the system.

Many business and digital issues and initiatives span many, if not most, of the eight core parts of every digital business system, especially over time.

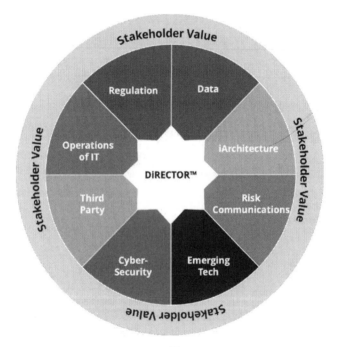

Figure 3—The DiRECTOR™ Framework © DDN LLC

System thinkers will conceptualize and understand the entire system along with its component parts, their interrelationships and how they fulfill the systems varied purposes.

Each of the eight domains making up a complex digital business system can be viewed as subsystems of the larger one, including:

Data — Digital systems start with data, and how the entire business system converts data into knowledge, insight, and action. Data and its enrichment as it evolves into actionable insight can directly drive many value propositions, in whole or in part.

It's the foundation upon which every digital business runs and is actively targeted by hackers for its intrinsic value.

iArchitecture — Information architecture comprises the technology design and parts that enable the digital system. Digital systems embody the software, network, business processes, and hardware components enabling and sustaining every digital business system.

Risk Communications — Crisis communication gets the headlines. But communication around digital business systems spans strategic, operational, and tactical communications that need to reach many stakeholders internally and externally. Digital risk disclosures and digital transformation change-management communications are frequent systems challenges for corporate leaders.

Emerging Technology — New digital tools are continually emerging that can enable, threaten, or redefine existing business value drivers. Additionally, these tools layer on new complexities across the existing system. They can also exploit or alter fundamental economic concepts and principles in new ways, making them an essential element in a complex digital business system.

Cybersecurity — Where there's business value, there's a risk. Hackers hack weakness, and complex, poorly secured digital systems offer them opportunity. The non-stop cybersecurity threat in every digital business system is in and of itself a demanding systemic risk challenge. Systems thinkers, from the boardroom down, view cybersecurity not as an afterthought, but as a multi-faceted and integrated component of every digital environment.

Third-Party — Business ecosystems have never been more connected internally or externally. Systemic issues compound across any extended business network that is continuously connected. Every third-party interacting with a digital system creates interdependencies and contagion risks across all systems, from regulators to business partners and service providers.

Operations of IT — The pace of change in digital and IT is unrelenting. The ability of an organization and its digital operations teams to effectively adapt to this type of dynamic environment plays a critical role in the entire system's sustainability, resiliency, and effectiveness.

The human part of complex systems is frequently where failure can occur that threatens the entire system. But it's often also where systemic risks can be stopped or controlled.

Regulation — Digital regulation is accelerating and expanding. Fines, penalties, and rules imposed by regulators directly influence businesses and shape their digital systems. Rules imposed by others beyond regulators, such as business partners and customers, make regulation a multi-stakeholder challenge and a vital element affecting the entire system.

The Key Causes of Systemic Risk

Strategic risk and operational risk in digital business systems are linked.

The digital tools that can deliver a new value proposition frequently offer new ways for hackers to target that value.

There are five primary contributors or causes of systemic risk in any digital business system. These are issues intrinsically raising the level of systemic risk embodied within the entire system and threatening its purpose. These factors heighten the strategic and operational risks of short and long-term digital value creation and preservation.

They are a part of the DiRECTOR™ framework, summarized by the acronym RISCX™.

Replaceability — How rare, irreplaceable and important is a component within the digital system? Critical, hard-to-replace components create significant risk and brittleness in a complex system.

The more dependent the system is on the component and the harder it is to replace, the greater the level of risk that part poses to the larger system.

Interconnectedness — Businesses and the world have never been more interconnected. Digital environments can be highly connected both internally and externally.

The more connection points across the system, the greater the risk of contagion, both inbound and outbound and the greater the risk of the failure spreading and cascading.

Size — Size impacts total exposure across the system. The larger the data universe being enabled, the more risk there can be within that data and across the system. Size is factored in from every perspective including number of end users, third-parties, software systems, etc.

Scale and breadth create more interconnections and more points of vulnerability, adding to digital complexity and contributing to systemic risk.

Complexity — Complexity in any environment makes it more difficult to understand how the environment functions and how it can be controlled. Digital complexity develops from multiple areas, including the number of component elements and heterogeneity within the system and operation.

The greater the number of different types of parts in the system, the higher the level of systemic risk within the system.

X-Jurisdiction — Rules are imposed from multiple sources in digital environments such as legal settings, contractual customer service levels or implicit constraints within the system's elements. Companies and networks spanning the globe create vulnerabilities *from* anywhere that can travel rapidly *to* everywhere.

The more jurisdictions and rules a digital system is exposed to, the more difficult it is to oversee and manage rules-based risk, and the higher the risk within the system.

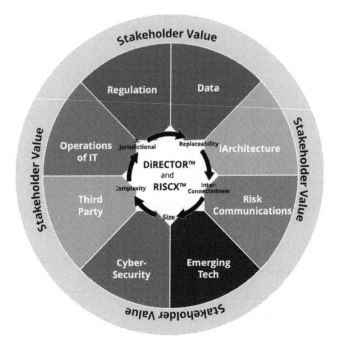

Figure 4—DiRECTOR™ and RISCX™ Models © DDN LLC

The Cybersecurity Free-Rider

For systems thinkers, there is a free-rider problem accompanying any complex system from a risk perspective. It relates to the concept that where value exists, there is inherent risk. There is a natural incentive in complex systems to skim the value created by those who haven't gone to the expense or effort of creating the system. That's exactly what hackers do.

In complex digital business systems, this explains why cybercrime is such a big business, and getting bigger, and why cybersecurity is so vital yet so difficult.

As systems become more complex, they naturally do so because they can deliver more value. But this offers more places for value to be extracted from the system by those who haven't gone to the time and effort of having developed the system.

Professor Joe Tranquillo of Bucknell and author of the book *An Introduction to Complex Systems*[30] explains it this way:

This goes back to some work by network theorists on hub-type networks—a random attack on a network has a very low chance of picking a hub, and therefore these networks are robust against random attacks.

But, a "smart" attack on a hub can bring down the entire system very quickly. Here is the catch; the systems that have the most to gain by tapping into the functions of a larger system, are in fact smaller systems that can skim off the top. These are individual hackers, viruses, terrorist groups, cancerous cells, small bands of thieves, and so on.

Small systems can take down large systems through targeting.

Once a vulnerability is found in a system, it often can be exploited in other ways. In the systems literature, this would be like one system "mapping out" another to probe for other vulnerabilities. Think of a thief who initially breaks in to steal food but then finds jewelry that's an easy grab and of more value.

It is a systems principle that when a large system finds and exploits value (usually by building functions to extract that value), a simple system can always come in and (without building up those functions itself) skim off some of the value.

This situation happens frequently in cybercrime. Hackers target vulnerable end points, such as a laptop computer, and then search out and find greater value in the network and larger system.

The perfect crime is the one passing undetected. An Advanced Persistent Threat (APT) enters a network and waits undetected, looking for value when it appears. Complex systems offer many points of entry, and more complicated environments help these stealthy risks thrive.

Hackers often also try to attack a small business partner, and then swim up-stream through trusted connections to find more value in a larger business. Highly connected extended business ecosystems intrinsically suffer from this type of systemic cybersecurity risk free-rider challenge.

So, what do the larger systems do to counter the threat of much smaller risks trying to exploit the larger system? Professor Tranquillo goes on to explain how this works in biology:

In the biological world, they build immunities, and these are usually based off the history of past attacks. Biological systems have two approaches to viruses and other irritants:

1) A fast-acting, very blunt (meaning it is not targeted and only works for a short time) and relatively simple response that has been evolved over a long period of time (the innate immune system, responsible for things like swelling, etc.). This system will kick into gear for almost any attack on the system (e.g. breaking a bone) and;

2) A more targeted, longer-lasting response that is created specifically for this particular attack.

As digital business systems evolve and take on more dynamic properties beginning to mirror the natural world, these biological risk response approaches may offer a new roadmap for mitigating cybersecurity risk.

"Herd immunity" is a concept talked about extensively during the COVID-19 pandemic. It means that when a significant number of people in a population have immunity, the "herd" acts as a direct mechanism slowing down the spread of a contagious virus. If 80% of a population has a virus, only two out of every ten people with whom any individual interacts could transmit it.

The same concept can and does work in cybersecurity.

Public-private partnerships and industry groups sharing information and working to stop vulnerabilities before they can spread are examples of how this practice moves from a biological world to the digital one. The herd, or larger group of defenders, has a stronger collective immunity against individual threats.

A business ecosystem possessing a high degree of third-party connectivity could consider such an approach. This reduces the weakest link threat and reduces the systemic cybersecurity risk inherent in interconnected business systems. This change would be a significant paradigm shift in how most companies approach cybersecurity threat detection and defense. The largest firms in a business ecosystem have the most to gain with this approach.

Other approaches will have to be considered to mitigate the long-term cybersecurity threat. One approach may involve looking at the problem differently, through the eyes of a systems thinker. While the natural inclination is to build stronger defenses, i.e., higher walls and larger moats that prevent hackers from entering the network, a systems thinker would view the problem differently.

They would see the complex system as inherently fallible and look to solve the problem another way. A general principle of any crime is that when the cost of stealing something is greater than the value of what the criminal is trying to steal, the item is secure. Traditional cybersecurity approaches raise the cost to hackers by making their boundaries harder to breach, causing the hacker to spend more time and effort on their attacks.

But a system thinker would see a breach as inevitable given the intrinsic traits of complex systems discussed previously. Because of this, a system thinker would think about making the target of a breach, the data, worthless to a hacker.

And some innovative cybersecurity companies are beginning to do just this. They are securing emails and data files with incredibly strong encryption methods to make the data worthless to the hacker. Even if a hacker can get to the data, they can't access it because of highly resilient encryption methods.

So, the incentive to the hacker has been eliminated by reducing the value of their crime to zero. The data has become secure by making it worthless to the hacker.

These approaches and many others will need to evolve into the complex digital world that serves our future.

We will see businesses fully embrace AI that fights back against threats automatically.

—Poppy Gustafsson, co-CEO Darktrace[31]

Cybersecurity risk won't go away post-pandemic.

It will escalate alongside the massive changes that will be taking place. Effective cybersecurity risk management is intrinsically systemic, a collection of disparate, interrelated activities focused on a common goal of protecting the digital value that companies create.

Unfortunately, there will be no flattening of the cyber-security risk curve in digital systems post-pandemic.

New risks and threats, even during periods of constructive change, usually outpace the ability to protect and defend against them.

But new approaches offer promise.

IDEA KEY CONCEPTS

⊃   Eight key parts in complex digital business systems work together to safely create and capture value in business: Data, iArchitecture, Risk Communications, Emerging Technology, Cybersecurity, Third-Party, Operations of IT and Regulation. These are as reflected by the acronym DiRECTOR™.

⊃   The key causes of systemic risk in complex digital business systems are: Replaceability, Interconnectedness, Size, Complexity and X-Jurisdiction that exist within each of the eight parts of the DiRECTOR™ model, as reflected by the acronym RISCX™.

⊃   Cybersecurity is a natural systemic risk in any complex digital system, and the complex system itself incentivizes targeted attacks.

IDEA IN PRACTICE

⊃   Train the corporate board and technology leadership team to speak the same language in digital and cybersecurity risk oversight using DiRECTOR™ and RISCX™. The conversation needs to be value-aligned and address the parts of the system and how they work together to safely deliver digital value.

➲ Look for new ways to strengthen cybersecurity defenses like a systems thinker would by leveraging collective security concepts or impairing the value of data to a hacker.

Chapter 5

Risk is a permanent condition of reality, and humans have been instinctual risk managers throughout history. Enterprise Risk Management (ERM) as a structured business management practice has been around for almost sixty years.

COSO—or the Committee of Sponsoring Organizations (www.coso.org)—has played a leading role in developing the practice of enterprise risk management, publishing its first Enterprise Risk Management - Integrated Framework in 2004.

Strengthening ERM 1.0

Their ERM framework coincided with the legislation known as Sarbanes-Oxley (SOX) which was in response to the financial reporting frauds at Enron, WorldCom and others. ERM was a big step forward in understanding and reducing risk for leaders and their organizations.

The business world has evolved considerably over the last several decades, especially technologically. The interdependence and interconnectedness of many of the world's business systems are unique in history.

In 2004, COSO defined ERM as a process "...designed to identify potential events that may affect the entity, and manage risks to be within its risk appetite..."[32]

Their definition focused on "events", which in practice became applied by estimating the financial impact of a risk (event) and appraising the probability of the event occurring. It could be reflected in the formula: *Risk = Probability x Impact*.

It doesn't reflect the compound impact of risk to the other system parts, or to the larger system. A very low-probability event with a potential high impact would calculate out to a low level of risk using that generally accepted formula.

The result of this event-level application is that frequently, the low-level risk would be accepted, and nothing would be done about it. In complex systems risk oversight and management, low-probability events cannot get ignored.

Their impact on the broader system must be understood before informed decisions about controlling them can be made.

That's the subtle, but very significant difference in approaching enterprise risk management as a systems thinker in a complex world.

COSO updated their framework in 2017 along with their definition of ERM:

The culture, capabilities, and practices, integrated with strategy-setting and performance, that organizations rely on to manage risk in creating, preserving and realizing value[33].

A useful definition, but one that would be better with the words "event and systems-level" inserted after the word "manage":

*The culture, capabilities, and practices, integrated with strategy-setting and performance, that organizations rely on to manage **event and systems-level** risks in creating, preserving and realizing value.*

That's a more accurate ERM 2.0 definition for a systems thinker in a complex world.

The DiRECTOR™ framework is designed to fix this shortcoming in typical ERM practice. It complements the COSO ERM model as a tool explicitly focused on understanding systemic risk in complex digital business systems. It can be integrated into any existing ERM approach.

The principles of complex systems science and thinking also extend to understanding how opportunity or strategic risk can start with an event, such as a change in consumer behavior, and flow across an entire company or industry.

Therefore, the objective of ERM for a systems thinker is digital value creation, capture *and* protection.

What's at Stake and What's the Risk?

Understanding and setting risk appetite levels and risk tolerances are two key responsibilities of any corporate board. These concepts relate to establishing the boundaries for the value that the company has at stake, and the risk to that stake.

Ford Inc. deciding to establish a US$10 billion space-exploration division would demonstrate that the corporate board of Ford has a large risk appetite and a high-risk tolerance.

Understanding risk appetite and risk tolerance are instinctual concepts for most executives with these kinds of big bets.

However, when it comes to systemic risk, instinct should be replaced by a structured approach that considers the intricate and interconnected nature of complex dynamic systems.

ISSUE IN ACTION: THE CASINO

A simple casino story illustrates the two critical issues of risk appetite and risk tolerance.

Every gambler makes a conscious or subconscious decision around these two issues when they walk into a casino to gamble. Two specific behaviors define every gambler's risk appetite and risk tolerance as they stroll the casino floor.

First, the amount of money the gambler is willing to bet indicates their risk appetite and second, the game they choose to play indicates their tolerance for risk.

Unlike business, casino games all have precise odds. A gambler who decides to play Keno has a high tolerance for risk as it has a house advantage that can reach 40%. A blackjack player has a lower tolerance for risk as that game only has a house advantage of between 1% -2%[34].

Most casual gamblers don't understand these odds, but the pros do. There is no more certain way to lose money in a casino than to not understand the risk of the game. Casinos work very hard to make sure that fun and easy bets have high risk levels, increasing the likelihood the gambler will find and make those bets and quickly lose their stake.

Business leaders don't have the luxury of not knowing the risks within the competitive games their companies are playing, or that exist in their digital system. They're paid to know what value is at stake and what the risk to that stake is. Neither is possible within their business if they don't understand complex systems risk.

In the Equifax story told in the next chapter, their leadership team may have thought they were playing a low-risk game with their digital system, when in fact the game was anything but and their entire business was at stake.

Many executives instinctually view risk mitigations as activities focused on preventing adverse outcomes, i.e., as a defensive undertaking. Activities like preventing a hacker from stealing sensitive corporate data or stopping fraud in financial reporting are common risk oversight and management priorities. That's right, but only half of the story.

Effective risk oversight and management also steers an organization into the future by optimizing an expected business outcome, e.g., revenue growth and profitability. Improving the likelihood of meeting a revenue growth objective or successfully executing on a strategic initiative to enter a new market are also crucial components of effective risk oversight and management.

Systemic change and the opportunity it brings, requires a similar way of thinking. Systemic change is about strategic or opportunity risk and how the complex digital business system creates stakeholder value in a rapidly changing world.

IDEA KEY CONCEPTS

⮑ Enterprise Risk Management as a practice needs to consider both event and systems-level risk to understand total risk in a complex world.

⮑ The DiRECTOR™ framework is additive to established ERM practices and focuses specifically on how systemic risk in complex digital business systems supports business value.

⮑ Business leaders need to understand risk appetite and risk tolerance within their digital systems to deliver business upside while protecting the downside.

IDEA IN PRACTICE

⮑ Map and align the digital portfolio and risk within the digital system to specific stakeholder value issues e.g., revenue growth, operating margin improvement, capital efficiency, employee productivity, employee wellbeing, customer satisfaction and retention, etc.

⮑ Expand the existing approach to ERM practices to understand and document systemic risk issues.

⮑ Apply systems thinking to the changes impacting markets and businesses to begin to understand systemic change and its opportunities.

Chapter 6

Complex systems are comprised of many interrelated parts. Collectively, they form a system that fulfills an intended purpose or function.

The healthcare system, financial system and business systems are examples. Systems can also have subsystems.

As leaders develop systems-thinking competencies, complex systems will come into focus everywhere.

Understanding how the parts relate and work together and how this behavior influences the system's performance is where understanding becomes difficult. But it's far from impossible.

Mapping complex systems is the starting point to understanding them.

Mapping a Complex Digital Business System

Mapping and understanding a complex digital business is not only possible, but it's also *necessary* to recognize the risks within the system. Systems thinkers and leaders will also use these principles to map and understand the changes that are impacting their business system post-pandemic.

Mapping a system helps identify its parts, their relationships and their interdependencies. It is also essential to identifying the intended system impact or the value driver it's facilitating or supporting.

To illustrate this, we've analyzed the Equifax data breach using the DiRECTOR™ framework. DiRECTOR™ is designed specifically to help leaders apply systems thinking to their complex digital business systems to understand how they safely drive value.

Frameworks are structured ways to analyze an issue or problem. They help to conceptualize and understand complex issues. They do not solve the issues that they may uncover, but they're the starting point to answers and solutions.

First, we've presented a narrative of the digital business environment and the systemic risks and failures leading to the Equifax data breach.

This is based on input from Graeme Payne, former Chief Information Officer of Global Corporate Platforms at Equifax, and the book he wrote on the subject[35].

Second, a systems map has been developed alongside the narrative, to visually illustrate the complex system, its various parts and how they relate.

There's one key point to remember about complex systems risk in analyzing the Equifax breach. It is that small events can have big impacts on complex systems.

Systems thinkers don't dismiss low-probability events. Instead, they understand how these interact with the broader system and only then can they make informed decisions about dismissing, mitigating or controlling them.

The Equifax data breach is a case study in complex systems breakdown and how a small error compounded with others to create a much bigger systems failure.

The Equifax Story

Founded in 1899, Equifax is one of the three large players in the credit reporting industry, along with Experian and TransUnion.

They're a "trusted steward" sitting between various data providers (banks, insurance companies, telcos, utilities, employers) and their revenue-generating customers who can often be the very same data providers.

Equifax is also a data company, converting raw data into meaningful and actionable insights.

The data that Equifax collects is used to develop scores, insights, marketing campaigns, and so on. This helps lenders make credit decisions, employers make hiring decisions, and lessors make leasing decisions.

Business Value — What's at Stake

Systems thinking around complex digital business systems first requires clarity around the digital system's function, and what's at stake.

The question, "What business value does the system support or serve?" is the starting point for a systems thinker.

Equifax is in the business of converting data into useful information.

The complex digital business system that Equifax built is their business, directly driving shareholder value, revenue, profitability and everything in between.

The digital business system powering the Equifax business model manages a staggering volume of data[36]:

RECORDS	YEAR 2017
Consumers	820 million
Businesses	91 million
Employee	278 million
Trade Accounts	5.75 billion
Public Records	201 million

The entire complex digital business that Equifax designed and built, supports, secures and serves every one of its stakeholders, from data providers to shareholders, to customers.

Their shareholders care primarily about how this system creates and protects shareholder value, i.e., stock price and dividends. Their consumers, employees, partners, suppliers and the communities within which they operate all value and care about different things.

Different subsystems within the overall Equifax digital system may be focused on one need, or many. A customer relationship management system may be focused on improving customer service and increasing account-level revenue, while other subsystems may be focused on raising employee productivity or understanding market trends and issues.

A Technology Debt That Came Due

In 1970, regulators started to pay attention to the power behind the data possessed by Equifax and other credit reporting providers. The Fair Credit Reporting Act (FCRA) was legislated by the FTC as a step toward protecting and developing consumer trust. It put a requirement in place on the credit providers to allow consumers to dispute potentially erroneous data in their credit reports.

Over time, additional regulatory requirements and bodies layered on complexities for Equifax when the Consumer Financial Protection Bureau was founded in 2011. The U.S. states would also begin to introduce regulation that impacted Equifax and this issue specifically.

In response to this regulatory requirement, Equifax needed to manage this process and the data they'd have to collect about their consumer inquiries and investigations. The Equifax IT operations team designed, built and deployed a system called the Automated Credit Investigation System or ACIS. To build it, they used the tools they knew; ones that they felt were best suited to the system's requirements at that time.

For over four decades, the Equifax IT operations and cybersecurity team supported and secured ACIS. Over a million people would be visiting the web portal every month by the time of the breach in 2017.

Initially, ACIS was built and used by internal call center employees. But eventually, the internet came along and ACIS was extended directly to the Equifax customer base through a web portal built using a common open-source piece of software called Apache Struts.

In 2003, the U.S. Department of Homeland Security's cybersecurity division founded the Computer Emergency Readiness Team, called US-CERT. One role of US-CERT is to coordinate with the private sector by disseminating cyber threat warning information. Private sector cybersecurity teams, including the Equifax team, work regularly with different government agencies—a critical risk communications activity that's a pivotal part of the entire digital system.

On March 8th of 2017, US-CERT sent a notification about a critical vulnerability in Apache Struts, the third-party open-source software that Equifax had integrated into their web portal for ACIS. Private sector firms monitored these important risk communications and reacted quickly to close these vulnerabilities, as did Equifax.

The Equifax threat and vulnerability team immediately notified key internal resources that a critical patch was needed for Apache Struts, to eliminate the vulnerability;

429 people received the email. But not everyone who needed to get it, did.

Patches were applied and the next day they also ran a system scan which did not identify any components utilizing Apache Struts. It would turn out that this scan failed to identify 100% of the instances of Apache Struts in their digital system.

A manual review for other Apache Struts instances was also conducted, and it was discovered that an ACIS portal did not have an up-to-date security certificate. You can see a security certificate by clicking the little lock next to any website URL in a web browser; it looks like this:

Without an up-to-date security certificate, their intrusion prevention/detection system couldn't decrypt and inspect the traffic flowing through their own system. Equifax was blind to the traffic moving across their system from the ACIS web portal to their servers.

It would turn out that this certificate had been out of date for over twelve months. Equifax hadn't had any visibility into the traffic from this portal to their servers since long before the March 8th US-CERT notification.

They were blind to who was coming to the web portal and what was going across the network. They retained lawyers, immediately launched an investigation, and informed the FBI.

Fast forward to August. Once the full scope of the breach was known by management, the CEO would notify the board on August 24th and 25th. And the breach would be made public on September 7th.

But back to July 29th, mid-investigation. On this date, they discovered that another sixty-seven digital security certificates were out of date. Their intrusion detection systems were blind to more network traffic than they initially thought, and they had been blind since the US-CERT notification in early March.

The Apache Struts door was still open, exposing their entire system and business. Despite acting promptly and running several control procedures including secondary ones such as the system scan and manual checks, they hadn't patched 100% of the Apache Struts vulnerabilities after receiving the US-CERT critical notification.

It wasn't until July 29th that they had full visibility into their network traffic. This is when they found suspicious activity, they could trace back to a Chinese IP address; it had begun back on May 13th. They only fully secured their systems on July 30th.

Eventually, they'd disclose the fact that almost 150 million consumers' data had been breached. In January 2020, Equifax settled a major piece of litigation at a minimum cost of US$1.38 billion, the most comprehensive recovery in U.S. history related to a data breach case[37]. The full cost of responding to the breach plus all litigation will push their costs above US$2 billion.

Looking at how these events unfolded, they would initially be traced back to a risk communications failure in a critical e-mail.

A weakness in their systems scanning tool that didn't work well with their ACIS legacy technology compounded this and further contributed to the system's weakness.

And then their out-of-date digital certificates prevented them from monitoring network traffic.

Several key parts of their overall digital system had failed. These failures compounded, creating a much larger risk and failure within the overall system, causing one of history's largest consumer data breaches. And their entire business was at risk, but they didn't know it.

And yet going back to 1970, the initial purpose and value of the ACIS system had been to improve consumer trust and transparency.

A Systems Thinkers' Visualization

Using the eight DiRECTOR™ framework domains, a systems map of this scenario can be constructed. Four stages of the map are represented to show its evolution. Each of the framework's domains is highlighted in **_bold italics_** as they come into play throughout the Equifax story.

Every complex system has its parts, interactions between the parts, and a purpose, all represented in the following system map. Interactions between the eight DiRECTOR™ framework domains are shown by arrows illustrating the flows or interactions between key parts.

For a systems thinker, a visual representation of the Equifax story going back to 1970 would start and center on the system's purpose.

This purpose, which as a result of the external regulatory force of the Fair Credit Reporting Act was to allow consumers to monitor their own credit data controlled by Equifax and other credit service providers.

The stakeholder in this case was the consumer, and **_Regulation_** from the FCRA was forcing the credit reporting industry to improve consumer confidence and trust.

This stakeholder value that the FCRA regulation was forcing Equifax to strengthen is illustrated in Figure 5 by an arrow pointing to the central consumer value box in the Stage 1 diagram.

However, **Cybersecurity** risk always threatens digital value so that is represented as well, by the down arrow as an indication of value that can flow—or be skimmed out of the system.

The DiRECTOR™ domains of **Regulation** and **Cybersecurity** and their interrelationships with the consumer as stakeholder or system beneficiary are represented in this Stage 1 diagram view:

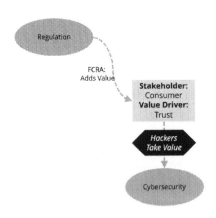

Figure 5—Stage 1 Equifax Digital Systems Map © DDN LLC

From here, to meet the new law's requirements, Equifax decided to build a software system called ACIS, or Automated Credit Investigation System, allowing its internal call center agents to collect the necessary data and manage the investigation process into consumer credit reports.

Stage 2 introduces the key elements of the Equifax complex digital business system responsible for creating, maintaining and securing the ACIS system that Equifax created.

ACIS would allow Equifax to manage the legal requirements with internal call center agents, delivering and protecting consumer value and trust as the law mandated.

New **Data** needed to be collected and the ACIS software system would need to be designed and built by their **IT Operations** team and then deployed into the Equifax **iArchitecture**.

Their **Cybersecurity** team would also need to secure the ACIS system.

At Stage 2, five of the eight DiRECTOR™ domains are involved and the system's complexity is coming into view as well as the interactions within the eight key subsystems of their digital system.

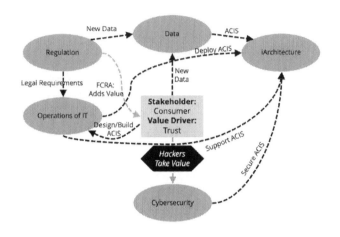

Figure 6—Stage 2 Equifax Digital Systems Map © DDN LLC

The five key causes of systemic risk from the RISCX™ model are also becoming clearer. Replaceability, interconnectedness, size, complexity and x-jurisdictional factors are starting to become identifiable as they raise the inherent level of risk within the entire system.

As a purpose-built system, ACIS wasn't easily replaceable along with the data that it was collecting and managing. This new system also needed to integrate within their existing IT environment. And it brought unique cybersecurity risks that not only added risk to this system but were also additive to the entire cybersecurity risk profile for the whole IT environment.

The ACIS system brought irreplaceability risk, and added size, complexity, new connections and new regulatory demands to the entire Equifax digital environment.

This type of systems map isn't unique to Equifax; the steps are like ones every company goes through to deploy a new software system. Each framework domain is a complex business function in and of itself. Integrating this system within the larger Equifax one compounds the risks to *every* system that Equifax supports and maintains.

In order to govern any complex digital business system, a corporate board needs to be competent in each of these eight DiRECTOR™ domains, as well as understand how the system works to fulfill its intended purpose.

Four decades rolled by with ACIS in place as technology innovations continued to evolve. The internet came along, and Equifax decided to add a web portal to ACIS to allow consumers to directly submit inquiries.

The **IT Operations** team built this interface using the **Emerging Technology** available to them at the time, including a common open-source **Third-Party** tool called Apache Struts.

This introduced two additional domains into the Equifax system; their complex digital systems map now looks like this at Stage 3:

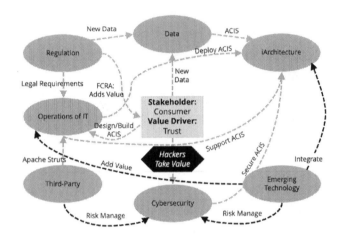

Figure 7—Stage 3 Equifax Digital Systems Map © DDN LLC

The digital systems map for just the ACIS subsystem within the Equifax digital environment clearly shows the complex interdependencies between the system's critical elements.

The final Stage 4 map in Figure 8, brings in **Risk Communications**, and illustrates the entire high-level ACIS systems map:

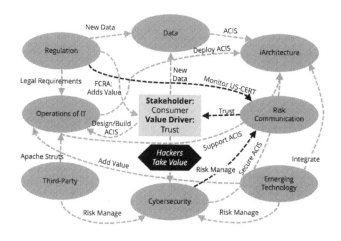

Figure 8—Stage 4 Equifax Digital Systems Map © DDN LLC

Risk Communications are not just crisis communications. They form a part of the entire digital business system from its inception and throughout its existence.

Regulatory disclosure requirements are increasing the demands on business leaders to identify and communicate key digital risks. The teams supporting and managing these systems throughout their lifecycle are also a critical part of the entire communications system, as Equifax would find out.

Risk communication involves every single stakeholder in the organization, including the board, every employee and all external stakeholders. Equifax would also have risk communication challenges and problems with their external stakeholders after the breach.

Being able to visualize the complexity of a system helps identify how it works to support its purpose and the critical risks within the system.

Risk cannot be mitigated unless it is first understood. Leaders need to be able to understand the value at stake with their digital business systems, and the inherent risks to that stake. Anything short of that is just "rolling the dice" and hoping that nothing goes wrong.

In a prior chapter, we used a casino and gambling metaphor to illustrate the issues of risk appetite and risk tolerance. Smart gamblers understand the risks of the games they play. Equifax might have been thinking they were playing a low-risk game, but in fact they were playing a very high-risk business game with their digital systems. Their entire business was at risk, and they didn't know it. It could have been much worse than a US$2 billion mistake for them.

This mapping exercise is intended to illustrate the business importance, risks and complexities of digital business systems. Designing, building, running and securing them is a multi-faceted challenge requiring deep expertise and coordination across a broad group of components making up the overall system. Not just once, but over time and in real time.

The DiRECTOR™ and RISCX™ frameworks are designed to help business leaders accomplish several objectives, all aligned to reduce the systemic risk levels inherent within their digital business systems.

They will help them:

1.   Understand the value drivers that complex digital business systems support and drive.

2.   Conceptualize the digital business system's complexity, its parts and how they work together.

3.   Understand critical issues or threats creating systemic risk within the larger system.

4.   Take informed action to mitigate key systemic risks within the system.

5.   Enable management and corporate directors to speak about and understand digital risk using a common framework and language.

6.   Train business leaders to think like systems thinkers to apply these key principles to the systemic challenges and opportunities facing their companies as a result of the pandemic.

BOB ZUKIS | PAUL FERRILLO | CHRIS VELTSOS

Chapter 7

Research in 2019 indicated that cyber-criminals cost the global economy US$2.9 million per minute in 2018[38]. Other estimates put the annual cost to the global economy at US$6 trillion by 2021[39].

Cybercrime is a big and profitable business, and it's only going to get bigger. Research puts the amount of revenue that cybercriminals take in every year at US$1.5 trillion[40], 3x the revenue of Walmart and almost 2x the revenue of Apple, Amazon, Microsoft, Tesla, and Facebook combined.

As more and more of the global economy runs through digital, what's at risk will only continue to go up. As the old joke goes, "Robbers rob banks because that's where the money is." Cybercriminals are stealing valuable intellectual property and financial assets, and businesses are being held hostage to ransomware because that's where the money is.

No sector is immune or without compromise; government and private sector networks and information are being exploited at an unprecedented scale by a growing array of state and non-state actors.

The cybersecurity war is being fought and lost on many fronts. And times of crisis only offer more easily exploitable opportunities. As businesses recover from COVID-19, the disruption and change due to take place will once again create gaping windows of opportunity that can be exploited by cybercriminals, now and far into the future.

Corporate directors are accustomed to overseeing a wide array of risks. So, what makes cybersecurity risk unique?

Cybersecurity is a subsystem of a complex digital business system and one of the eight parts of the DiRECTOR™ framework for understanding systemic risk in complex digital business systems. Cybersecurity is a collection of activities working together to effectively defend against a very smart, creative and active adversary every minute of every day. Other characteristics making cybersecurity a unique challenge include:

- The cybersecurity threat landscape expands and changes frequently and quickly.
- Risk is systemic, meaning a small failure can jeopardize the broader system.
- There's a high level of complexity in understanding the impact of risks.
- It's challenging to mitigate cybersecurity risk across diverse technologies.

- It's not just a technology issue. People and process are an important part of the system.
- What's at stake is increasing in value as business dependency on digital systems grows.

Much like COVID-19 brought the global economy to a very slow crawl, a cyber-risk event starting on one desk of an organization (or in a partner's) can, in a matter of hours, wreak havoc across the entire organization. And like fighting a pandemic, battling cyber attackers requires companies to be able to test for infection (detect intruders), isolate and treat infected individuals (scrutinize systems/networks affected), and restore patients' health (remediate the damage).

Unlike other risks regularly tracked and discussed in boardrooms for decades, cyber risk is also a relative newcomer and few board members have relevant experience or training to help them understand and oversee its risks. It's not just enough for board members to ask questions, as the questions are useless if corporate directors don't understand the answers.

Cybersecurity failures can spring from human error, over-reliance on technical controls, and failing to test the resilience of interconnected and interdependent systems. A lack of planning and unpreparedness for abstract *what-if* scenarios and threats is also common.

Most companies and boards probably don't understand the cybersecurity risk level inherent in their complex digital business systems, or what's at stake because of that risk. Thus, they're likely not applying the concepts of risk appetite, or knowing what's at stake—and risk tolerance, or knowing what the risk to the stake is. It's impossible to effectively govern or manage cybersecurity risk without knowing these two fundamental issues.

Driving in a Snowstorm

Imagine driving in a snowstorm. Your objective is to get to your destination safely. The risk of not getting to your destination safely—such as ending up in a ditch—is dependent upon several factors such as the technical aspects of your car (steering, brakes, dashboard indicators all working correctly), your own driving habits (safe distance, safe speed, gentle handling) and the road conditions themselves.

To make this scenario an accurate metaphor for cybersecurity risk, there would also need to be another car trying to run you off the road, rocks that would unexpectedly fall onto the road, a screaming child in the backseat, and you'd need to arrive at your destination on time or face significant financial loss.

That's the challenge every company faces in defending the digital value they create.

ISSUE IN ACTION: SWIFT Banking

SWIFT stands for the "Society for Worldwide Interbank Financial Telecommunications," a communications system for member banks that was set up in 1973. SWIFT's purpose was to allow funds transfer between the banks and other financial institutions, including the Federal Reserve. Prior to SWIFT, its functions were handled via Telex.

This global system is used every day between its nearly 11,000 members in 200 countries, efficiently transferring over US$5 trillion in funds daily[41]. Over 38 million messages went through SWIFT daily in March 2020. Transfers are made using specific bank identifying codes.

As a complex system, its many parts are its interconnected members, and its purpose is to safely, securely and quickly enable large fund transfers in the financial sector.

As a complex digital business system, it handles a massive amount of critical data daily. Its architecture needs to be resilient and reliable in real-time. The IT and cybersecurity operations teams need to be rapidly responsive to issues, and the system needs to be extremely secure given the amount of money it moves.

These cyber defenses would be tested in 2015-2016 and would fail.

Using stolen credentials from Bangladesh Central Bank employees, criminal hackers caused more than three dozen fraudulent money transfers—to the value of $81 million—from the U.S. Federal Reserve into hacker-controlled bank accounts.

By the time the Bangladesh Central Bank figured out what had happened, the money was gone despite many warnings from the Federal Reserve to the bank asking, "Were these transactions ok?"

They were not.

Given what's at stake within the SWIFT system, there should be a low level of risk tolerance to any cybersecurity threats to the system. This would translate to the system being incredibly strong against threats and attacks so that fraudulent transactions wouldn't occur, so members could have a high level of trust in the SWIFT system.

But SWIFT had some critical risks in their cybersecurity management system, creating this larger scale failure. They did not prioritize access to the network. There was also not an anomaly detection system at the bank to catch the three dozen transfers. They also lacked multi-factor authentication for network access to guard against stolen credentials being used to execute money transfers. Very basic, yet critical points of risk introducing systemic risk into this key financial system.

Secondary controls were also non-existent as the bank did not get the warning from the Federal Reserve to verify that the transactions were valid.

A 2016 Office of Financial Research (OFR) report concluded:

This incident showed the ability of cybersecurity intruders to bypass complex business controls. It also showed that cybersecurity threats require responses at the end-user and the system level[42].

The OFR report also stated:

This increase in digital links also gives rise to financial stability risks. A cybersecurity incident that disrupts a large firm could trigger second-order effects. For example, a large troubled firm could

> *default on obligations to counterparties or impair market liquidity[43].*

The after-the-fact analysis of the SWIFT hack called out the larger risks to the system. It's not unusual for the importance of understanding systemic risk to be regularly identified during after-the-fact analysis of breach situations.

In hack after hack, bad actors continue exploiting vulnerabilities in complex systems.

Hackers were able to micro-target their way into the massive SWIFT system and skim a large amount of value from it. Hackers understand these opportunities and how bad almost every company is at understanding and mitigating systemic risk. That's why their business is thriving.

Leaders need to become as good as the hackers in understanding these risks and take the steps to control them.

The One Cybersecurity Leadership Question

Corporate boards frequently ask management if the company is spending the right amount of money on cybersecurity.

It's the wrong question because it lacks context. That context is value and understanding risk appetite and risk tolerances. Or what's at stake and what the risk to the stake is. Only then can an informed decision be made in deciding what it's worth spending in order to protect it.

Benchmark spending in cybersecurity is largely meaningless for this reason.

The right question is, "What's the value of what we are trying to protect, and how safe is it for what we're spending?"

Every company has a unique digital footprint creating value specific to the organization. And every company has a unique risk profile given their overall digital environment. What that value is worth and the risk to that value, relates only to that organization.

Post-pandemic, cybersecurity spending is also only going to go up, because the value at stake is increasing. Even during the pandemic, cybersecurity spending is increasing faster than other IT priorities.

An April 2020 survey of senior IT leaders indicated that 62% were increasing their cybersecurity spending. While this was in response to the increase in risk due to the scale of work-from-home initiatives, the longer-term trend should follow the increase in digital value that companies create[44].

Effective cybersecurity risk management is itself a very complex subsystem.

One weak link in the system, such as an employee clicking on a phishing email, can bring the entire business system to a halt.

Cybersecurity is a collection of disparate online and offline activities working together toward the collective purpose of protecting business value. Hackers take advantage of this, searching for and attacking the weakest link.

During times of distraction, as companies are experiencing with COVID-19, hackers see opportunity. During times of change and transformation, new vulnerabilities appear that hackers exploit faster than the defenders can protect.

Companies were not exactly winning the old cyber-security war. The systemic, post-pandemic changes demand a new cybersecurity approach as the cyber-security war is only getting started.

This new approach needs to start at the top of the organization. With a view that cybersecurity is a system designed and built to protect a complex digital business and the value it creates.

Zoom: Systemic Change and New Risk

One of the most talked about—and most relied upon—pieces of technology during many months in 2020, has been the video collaboration tool called Zoom. While video chat and video conferencing tools have been around for nearly two decades, the COVID-19 work-from-home crisis has propelled huge swaths of the workforce—teachers, students, doctors, patients, office employees, business leaders, lawyers—into becoming remote workers.

Prior to founding Zoom, Eric Yuan was working for a competing collaborative conferencing product, WebEx, which he remarked was focused on a rather narrow set of use cases[45], e.g. share and narrate a presentation at a distance. In 2011, he pitched an idea[46] for what would then morph into Zoom to Cisco executives, Cisco having acquired WebEx some four years earlier. Yuan pitched a video-rich, smartphone-friendly collaborative and multi-platform app[47]. When Cisco turned him down, Yuan set off to secure funding and start Saasbee, whose name would, a year later, be changed to Zoom Video Communications, Inc.

Zoom continued to gain users and market share, and on April 18th, 2019, celebrated with much fanfare as it achieved an initial public offering (IPO).

Zoom's path to success wasn't set in stone. Even in 2011, the field of videoconferencing and collaborative conferencing had many solid players with large user bases and established name-brand weight. Yet Zoom's leaders saw an opportunity to disrupt those market leaders and make a niche for itself. They saw new territory. What they didn't know was whether the opportunity would be a Cool Blue Lake, or a Deep Blue Ocean.

The Zoom team recognized that social, technological and demographic external forces were changing, yet the world of collaborative conferencing was staying static. It was not responding to their view of evolving market needs and wants.

Zoom's profound understanding and belief in these external forces would be richly rewarded as they collided with the new engagement behaviors changed by the pandemic. Their user growth would explode from ten million users in December 2019 to over 300 million at the end of April 2020[48].

As it seemed like half the world was switching to Zoom in the first quarter of 2020, cybersecurity and privacy experts started probing their data and privacy issues. Reports of "Zoombombing," when unwanted and unauthorized individuals virtually crashed into a meeting, would frequently result in chaos, frustration, and offended participants.

By the end of April 2020, there were nearly one million news results for "Zoombombing."

The issue of Zoombombing was in part due to how easy it was to set up a Zoom-based meeting. Sign-in, click on the *New Meeting* button, and voila, you get a web link that you can share with anyone, and it also comes with dial-in numbers for those needing to call in.

Those same meeting participants would then share the links widely, such as posting the links on discussion boards, Facebook chats, and even, in some cases, their website. Zoom's ease of use also meant that most did not take the time to limit participants, to stage participants in a virtual waiting room, or to add a password to protect the Zoom meeting.

The opportunity presented by systemic change and their new markets moved faster than their cybersecurity system did to control these new risks. Risks that only opened because of the unique value their technology was designed to offer.

By the end of April, Zoom had worked with businesses large and small, school systems, government agencies, and deployed improved default meeting options. They also embarked on a risk communications effort to raise user awareness of the dangers of sharing meeting information too widely.

However, Zoom's privacy and security-related troubles were only beginning. Probing questions surfaced about whether Zoom was sending meeting data to other countries, who else had access to its source code, whether confidential-level meetings were adequately protected, whether the app spied on its users—with one report that it spied on other programs in use during a Zoom meeting.

Google, SpaceX, Standard Chartered, NASA, the German Foreign Ministry, the Australian Defence Force, all of Taiwan's government agencies, and schools in New York City and Singapore would all ban the use of Zoom[49].

The external forces creating Zoom's Deep Blue Ocean threatened to sink the very opportunity it had presented.

Zoom's cybersecurity team has since managed to not only accommodate the large rise in users, from ten million to over 300 million in 3 months[50], but it's also managed to improve the app's security and the privacy of the information it shares.

Zoom's CEO himself has posted regular updates, such as the one on their 90-day plan to improve privacy and security[51] and weekly progress report updates[52].

Most parts of the DiRECTOR™ framework for understanding systemic risk in complex digital systems came into play during Zoom's experience. Data, iArchitecture, Risk Communication, Cybersecurity and IT Operations were all vital subsystems that worked together to allow them to respond to the paradigm-shifting online engagement forces of change offered to them and that they were uniquely positioned to capitalize on.

The mind and observations of their CEO before the pandemic were acutely tuned to new needs, wants and behaviors of a marketplace, one that's quickly become a massive COVID-19 delivered Deep Blue Ocean.

THE GREAT REBOOT and the DiRECTOR™ framework are similarly intended to prepare the minds of all business leaders to understand the systemic opportunities and risks COVID-19 brings.

IDEA KEY CONCEPTS

➲ Cybersecurity risk isn't like other business risks given its systemic complexity and real-time dynamics.

➲ Corporate boards need the skills and competencies to oversee all aspects of a complex digital business system.

➲ Cybersecurity risk needs to be understood in the context of the business value at stake.

➲ Opportunities from systemic change post-pandemic will create new cybersecurity risks.

➲ As more value drives through digital, the costs of protecting that value can be expected to go up.

IDEA IN PRACTICE

➲ Boards should ask their CISOs to align their cybersecurity risk reports to the value of what's being protected by their cybersecurity activities and how secure that value is for what they're spending.

➲ Add cybersecurity competencies to the boardroom skills matrix and add corporate directors who understand all DiRECTOR™ domains.

Chapter 8

A Deep Blue Ocean Appears

I t will likely be said in the future that the coming of age of telepresence happened during the COVID-19 global pandemic of 2020.

Through a convergence of COVID-19 induced external forces and new behaviors, massive new marketplaces have opened for tools that enable and empower remote real-time interactions. Not just video-conferencing tools, but technology that can augment reality and empower remote engagement in new ways.

One company in Vancouver, Washington, RealWear, Inc., was also in the right place at the right time and is an early beneficiary of these forces. Their corporate board Chairman, Andrew Chrostowski shares their journey of the systemic changes impacting their business as a result of COVID-19.

With full disclosure, Andrew has joined the authors in developing and advancing the practice and profession of digital and cybersecurity risk oversight in the corporate boardroom. He also has a Master of Science, Systems Management from the USC Marshall School of Business and has been trained as a systems thinker.

His work with us at the forefront of digital risk oversight and his leadership at RealWear have converged to make him one of the first boardroom systems thinkers navigating the waves of systemic change being brought about by COVID-19.

The RealWear Story

This is RealWear's story through the perfect storm of COVID-19, as told by Andrew.

***

With COVID-19, corporate boards have never faced such a convergence of risks hitting them at the same time. While there have certainly been cybersecurity crises recently, the risks and failures from the pandemic have been hitting companies from every direction, and in a short amount of time.

Boards of both "essential" and "non-essential" businesses have been faced with immediate human and business-level survival issues. We've had to protect our employees, service customers, stay liquid, continue operations, ward off new cybersecurity threats, respond to economic upheaval and new regulations...all at the same time.

As social distancing, stay-at-home orders, and travel restrictions quickly emerged, companies had to first keep their employees connected so they could still do their jobs.

In response, there was a rapid and accelerated deployment of remote collaboration tools such as Microsoft Teams, Cisco WebEx, Slack and Zoom. Daily users of these tools skyrocketed. Suddenly, all these new risks were appearing and "Zoombombing" became a thing, with unauthorized hacks into video meetings.

Face-to-face discussions were replaced with video-meetings. Collaboration expanded to use rich-threaded messaging, and training was replaced with webinars. These activities all fall into what can be called telepresence, and while they existed before, they're now at the center of every business and used at scale.

As a board member and systems thinker, it's been fascinating to be in the middle of this. From a business value perspective, these tools have been a lifeline for many companies. They've enabled the most basic business value driver of them all, the ability of companies to keep functioning and to stay connected with their markets. I can't imagine what would have happened if these tools hadn't been available.

While some people used these tools before, their mass adoption is creating permanent shifts in human behavior with a willingness and desire to integrate them everywhere. For CEOs and directors, all the elements and risks inherent in complex digital business systems came into play as the massive effort to deploy telepresence technologies became a critical part of keeping companies running.

Businesses needed to ensure there was broadband internet connectivity, and these tools needed to integrate with their existing infrastructure. They had to rapidly assess how all these new access points and applications could compromise their data integrity and the security of their networks. Communications with employees to teach them how to use these tools while they were deployed, and then how to use them once that happened, were crucial. Even corporate board meetings and shareholder meetings had to move to these technologies.

IT and cybersecurity operations teams were working overtime to implement these tools and secure them, many of which were new to both them and their employees. With Zoom, third-party risks also came into play with their security issues.

Companies now have an enormous amount of data and information flowing through these new systems. It was— and remains—a systemic challenge and risk of epic proportions. Risks emerged that weren't fully understood, because the tool needed to be deployed quickly to keep companies functioning, which took priority.

All of this was happening at RealWear too, but industrial presence for first-line workers is our business. Our industrial clients faced the same issues with an additional challenge. How to accomplish this collaboration and knowledge transfer with frontline or first-line workers? The jobs worked by these key employees are not done in the comfort and safety of a home or office. They're done in warehouses, plants, factories, installations, and even hospitals. These users typically require PPE and the ability to use their hands freely for tools or equipment adjustments.

The use cases most commonly experienced during this pandemic involved getting around travel restrictions and ensuring facility access for service technicians to support equipment repair, training and medical services.

Unplanned downtime is expensive, and in critical healthcare situations, can be lethal. Having a local technician reach out to a remote expert who can collaborate real-time to solve locally to reduce downtime is a huge value driver in business, and even more important in healthcare.

During a time when automotive plants were converting production lines to produce ventilators, and clothing companies were creating face masks, rapid training of employees has been crucial. And because employees are unavailable due to sickness, isolation or travel restrictions, expertise is often marooned far from the point of production.

Extending the benefits of telepresence to these workers safely and hands-free requires a purpose-built wearable computer. RealWear, Inc. has been deploying a voice-controlled, Android computer to industry since 2016 and has grown to become the leading provider in the world.

The HMT-1 and HMT-1Z1 (intrinsically safe) devices allow industrial users to operate the equivalent of an Android tablet using only their voice up to 95 dB noise levels. Telepresence applications, workflow software, training videos and materials, as well as blueprints and work instructions are all available in a heads-up display.

And during this, our teams are also on the pandemic's frontlines helping medical first responders. RealWear technology is compatible with PPE such as hard hats, bump caps, hearing protection, and N95 respirators and surgical masks, the latter creating a new market in the medical field for wearable computers like the RealWear HMT-1. This market's potential has begun to be recognized through these pandemic accommodations, and it's a massive one spanning multiple sectors.

During the early COVID-19 days, HMT-1 devices were used in conjunction with an infrared camera to conduct thermal screening of people in crowded areas. Three separate hospitals in China used HMT-1 devices worn by a junior doctor in the isolation ward to two-way real-time consult with a senior physician. This increased their capacity to treat patients and reduced the critical constraint of physician capacity during the pandemic. Leverage like this is of critical value to healthcare systems worldwide.

Hands-free thermography helps screen for elevated body temperatures possibly indicative of fever presence, all while allowing the screener to be mobile and protected. Airports and essential businesses have been scanning travelers and consumers, but anywhere people gather has now become a market for this technology.

Will additional new markets open for this type of screening in spots such as restaurants, movie theatres, grocery stores or bars?

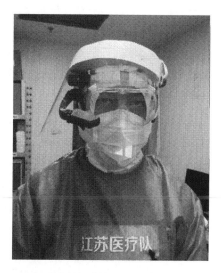

A physician in China wearing HMT-1.

Within the first six weeks of March, purchases of HMT-1 wearable computers that supported the COVID-19 battle increased to 35% of sales. The challenges of managing the pandemic led existing and new customers alike to accelerate their adoption of telepresence solutions for frontline and first-line workers.

As our client's executives and board members conducted virtual board meetings and ran their businesses remotely, the need to explain the benefits of knowledge transfer to connected industrial workers vanished. They were living our value proposition in real time.

A new paradigm in human behavior has been established out of the necessity for rich, and deeply engaging remote connectivity. While this want and need is obvious in healthcare because of the pandemic, these behaviors are spreading and will continue to spread across many industries.

The broader system supporting a real time high-reliability augmented-reality experience will also be even stronger with 5G, and eventually 6G.

The opportunities get bigger the more that I apply my systems-thinking competencies to them, as I reimagine how we interact and what we can do with these types of tools. But as a corporate board member, I'm also very aware of the systemic risks existing within our complex digital system as a business, and the systems we deploy with our customers. And we're doing things never done before—because they weren't possible.

I'm proud of the role that RealWear and our teams are playing in helping the world with the pandemic. While many people lost their battle against this virus, we're hopefully a part of keeping this number as low as possible.

I'm optimistic for what's to come, based on what we've learned from this time.

Andrew Chrostowski
Chairman of the Board and Acting CEO
RealWear Inc.

***

The External Forces Driving RealWear

Andrew summarized the external forces driving systemic change for RealWear pre- and post-COVID-19 using the STEEPLED model.

SOCIAL	
Pre-COVID	Post-COVID
Skepticism from business leaders on the value of telepresence.	Leadership was sold once they started living the use case daily. Extending this capability to their front-line workers makes clear sense.
We were pushing a use case and identifying sector relevancy.	Users are now identifying new applications across verticals and accelerating adoption.
Adoption and training were a "push" model.	Users now "pull" training to enable them to do their jobs.
TECHNOLOGICAL	
High dependencies on existing infrastructure, sometimes creating deployment barriers.	Barriers have been reduced for us as companies have expanded and strengthened connectivity.
Enterprise process and procedure dominate and slow deployments.	Creative problem solving dominates as users look for ways to get around barriers to deployment to get work done.

ECONOMIC	
Long consultative sales cycle.	Taking orders as demand explodes.
Some skepticism around the value proposition. Discussion revolved around ROI.	Post COVID-19 it's no longer an ROI question. These mission critical jobs could no longer be done at all without remote expertise.
ENVIRONMENTAL	
No real influence.	Threat of viral infection in the workplace, adds to our virtual value proposition long-term.
POLITICAL	
No real influence.	Travel restrictions imposed between countries and mandatory quarantine periods make remote service capability a necessity.
LEGAL	
No significant issues.	Liability related to disease transmission is leading companies to impose restrictions on workplace access solutions need to be compatible with PPE.
DEMOGRAPHIC	
Enthusiasm for the technology is highest in younger workers.	Familiarity and comfort gained with telepresence spans all age ranges and demographics now.

Chapter 9

The corporate director's role has never been more challenging, or vital.

Corporate directors had a difficult job before COVID-19 and they've been challenged like never during the crisis. Yet it's going to get even more demanding post-pandemic.

The corporate board is a critical part of every company's overall business system. Its role is not just value preservation, but value creation.

It too, like every other system and subsystem that will be rethought as a result of COVID-19, should be reconsidered to align with future needs.

Governing Complex Systems

In the United States, the last major reboot, or structural policy reform impacting the corporate boardroom came about as a result of the financial markets meltdown and financial reporting scandals of the early 2000's. New listing requirements from the NYSE and NASDAQ, the rise of governance ratings agencies, stricter judicial opinions and The Sarbanes-Oxley Act (SOX) of 2002 drove a paradigm shift in corporate governance aimed at restoring trust in public corporations.

In response to the financial reporting crises of the time, SOX drove major corporate governance reform. It impacted board composition, structure, disclosure and transparency, director independence and audit practices.

One specific thing that SOX forced, for the first time, was for corporate boards to have a Qualified Financial Expert (QFE) on the board. In hindsight, it's incredible to think that as recently as 2002, it was a novel concept in America's boardrooms to have the presence of a corporate director capable of understanding a financial statement. It took regulation, through SOX, to change that.

Board reform and capability always lags market developments. The COVID-19 crisis won't drive a regulatory sledgehammer to America's corporate governance practices as its corporations aren't to blame. But that doesn't mean boards can't and shouldn't evolve into the changes taking place.

And the area in which they need to evolve most critically is the one that's the most vital to their post-pandemic ability to thrive. It's their ability to effectively oversee and govern the complex digital business systems that will help their companies shape and safely navigate the future.

There has already been a strong desire for regulators to strengthen cybersecurity governance in America's boardrooms. This issue is clearly in the public interest, and regulators will eventually force reform. Regulators have already proposed rules ranging from the disclosure of cybersecurity skills for directors on the board, to data privacy laws with much stricter penalties and clear accountability for the board and CEO on these issues.

The unprecedented $5 billion fine the FTC imposed on Facebook[53] for their data privacy shortcomings forced a data privacy committee onto their board, third-party audits of their practices and CEO sign-off, a very SOX-like response.

This forced legal directive was far from a corporate governance innovation as the toy brand Hasbro—that makes the Mr. Potato Head doll—has had a data privacy committee on their board for several years.

Post-Pandemic Board Development

Most of America's corporate boardrooms haven't been responsive to the digital economy's evolution and risks. A few boards have adopted practices that keep up, such as adding corporate directors with deep and broad digital and cybersecurity backgrounds.

Some have even organized their digital risk oversight practices in the boardroom through a Technology & Cybersecurity Committee. Leaders such as Walmart, AMEX, Pfizer and FedEx have adopted this approach. Far from breakthroughs, they're common-sense developments.

And they are now table stakes to navigate the massive changes and risks of the pandemic and its aftermath as each company's complex digital business system is critical to its post-pandemic reboot. Disruption and change of this magnitude needs a focused approach, which is one key benefit of the committee structure in the boardroom.

A Technology & Cybersecurity Committee on public company boards is the perfect place to task a new generation of digital directors with this daunting oversight responsibility. Leading practices for the Technology & Cybersecurity Committee's oversight responsibility frequently cover:

- Alignment of business strategy, IT and enterprise architecture;
- Business continuity and disaster recovery;

- Cybersecurity risk, insurance and Directors & Officers liability;
- Cyberthreat intelligence;
- Data privacy and information lifecycle management;
- Device management policy;
- IT investment and strategy;
- IT service delivery;
- IT project prioritization, implementation and portfolio management;
- IT skills and capability management and organization structure;
- IT hardware/software lifecycle management;
- New and emerging technologies;
- Regulatory policy advocacy and management;
- Risk communications;
- Social media monitoring and engagement;
- Third-party IT vendor and service risk management.

The scope of effective digital and cybersecurity risk oversight is vast, too large of an agenda to assign to the full board or to include within any other committee as an afterthought.

While many corporate boards task their audit committee with cybersecurity risk oversight, that practice probably does more harm than good, as it would rarely give the issue the focus or skills it needs within an already very busy audit committee agenda. This creates a false sense of security that a low-risk cybersecurity game is being played, when the opposite is probably more likely.

Corporate directors are a critical part of every company's first-response team in strategic and operational risk, and leadership is a critical part of its digital business system.

Corporate boards can take several simple, yet transformative steps to immediately reboot their ability to deal with the extraordinary post-pandemic opportunities and risks:

1. Either expand the board, or through director succession add two or three digital directors possessing broad competencies necessary to oversee the entire complex digital business system. (The DiRECTOR™ framework can be used as a competency model);

2. Adopt a Technology & Cybersecurity Committee staffed with these directors who are joined by a multi-committee director from the audit committee;

3. Regularly bring in external experts as decision support or to keep the board current on emerging digital trends and issues, as well as post-pandemic market changes.

Several other common-sense board reforms can also help directors and the board deal with an increased director workload and higher needs and expectations into the post-pandemic future:

1.   Limit directors to no more than two public company board seats.

2.   Raise director compensation while increasing the expectation for director time from the current average of 245[54] hours a year.

3.   Invest in annual director development and education for the full board, developing directors' critical competencies in digital and cybersecurity risk oversight and staying current while also developing systems-thinking and governing competencies.

Chapter 10

To say this is a difficult time for business leaders understates the dire consequences of a global pandemic that's already cost the lives of many global citizens.

COVID-19 has been a perfect storm. A convergence of systemic risks and failures that's cascaded and impacted us all.

But the storm will pass.

What we do once we're in calmer waters will determine if the price paid by so many was in vain.

It's up to us to make sure that it isn't.

The future we imagined for 2030 has been pulled forward to the present.

—Tobias Lütke, CEO Shopify[55]

The opportunity that leaders and all of us have is to fix the systems that failed us. Not just to fix them for the few, but for the many. The virus doesn't discriminate, and the only way to defeat an enemy that knows no borders is with a collective defense; a united immunity.

This immunity starts with understanding our complex systems better, starting with our healthcare system, but not stopping there.

We know our systems have many strengths, but their vulnerabilities have proven overpowering. But we know we can fix them and make them better.

The best collective immunity is to understand the complex world we occupy—both its natural systems and the ones we've created—and to wake up to the realization that they can easily fail, with catastrophic consequences.

These complex systems serve and provide us with many wonderful things, but they are too fragile.

We need to recognize our leadership and actions have a critical role to play in how they perform and sustain us. We need to take steps to understand them, control them and make them stronger.

Hopefully, there's a new appreciation for what is at stake.

The modern business remains an incredible engine that's reshaped the world for the better over the last century. So, it's here where the reboot needs to start.

No business leader ever expected they'd live in a world where the only channel of engagement with employees, customers, suppliers and shareholders would be digital, but here we are.

Our digital systems stood out during the pandemic; they didn't fail. They're delivering us through it.

And while we'll get back to face-to-face interactions and communities, our digital operating systems are what can continue to move us forward. During the pandemic, they kept us operating, communicating and collaborating as humans and as businesses, albeit at a reduced level of functionality. They were our run-flat tire.

We need and want the value our digital systems bring, but they can do more, a lot more. They can also do it more creatively and safely. They can be, and are, the tools that will safely deliver the future. They're the tools that will continue to support, sustain and meet the diverse needs of a global population approaching eight billion fellow citizens of earth.

We know we can safely harness their power and the potential of systemic change, if we become better systems thinkers.

Becoming a Systems Thinker and Leader

We wrote THE GREAT REBOOT to strengthen the critical bond between business leaders and their understanding of complex systems. And we started by reinforcing the link between business leaders and the complex digital business systems that will shape and safely secure their digital futures.

Complex systems themselves are simple in concept but challenging in application. Complex systems have:

1. Parts;

2. Connections; and

3. An intended purpose.

Business leaders need to move forward balancing the opportunities of systemic change with the inherent risks of a complex world.

Like the general concepts of complex systems science, the roadmap for leading massive systemic risk and change is also straightforward—ABC.

This roadmap has three stages designed to address both the upside of complex systemic change and the flip side, managing the risks inherent within it.

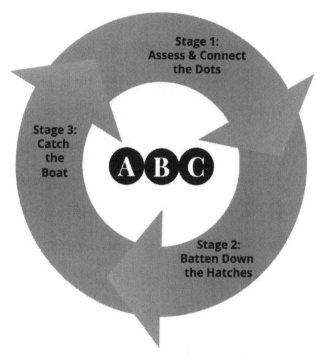

Figure 9—ABC (Assess, Batten & Catch) © DDN LLC

The ABC stages of the roadmap are to *Assess & Connect the Dots*, *Batten Down the Hatches* and *Catch the Boat*.

The roadmap reflects the stages for both the upside of systemic change and the downside of protecting digital risk.

The following graphic illustrates these concepts in action:

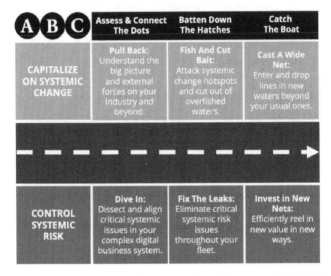

Figure 10—The ABC's of Post-Pandemic Success © DDN LLC

Stage 1 — Assess & Connect the Dots

To understand systemic change, business leaders need to pull back and assess the big and small changes driven by social, technological, economic, environmental, political, legal, ethical and demographic shifts. New behaviors and needs and wants will influence how these factors interact and flow across different complex business systems.

It's not paint-by-numbers, but it is literally connecting the dots. And it's not constrained to just existing industry environments. Leaders need to look beyond their sectors and consider impacts and opportunities far beyond their typical strategic horizons.

At the same time, a new appreciation for how your own complex digital business system functions and supports the value-generating initiatives of your business needs to be established. The goal is to understand how that digital system supports the changing value drivers throughout your business, and what the risk is to them at all levels of value creation for every stakeholder.

Stage 2 — Batten Down the Hatches

Change will be fast and furious as market disruptions take hold; it's already started. Critical systemic weaknesses in your digital operating system and business more broadly will need to be fixed before moving ahead.

Strategic decisions to exit or enter markets and new product offerings or services will need to be implemented quickly. Massive systemic changes are impacting entire sectors, some positively, but others negatively. Many small changes will offer opportunity while presenting new risks.

It won't be an easy reboot, as systemic change never is.

Corporate leaders and board directors can leverage the DiRECTOR™ framework to gain confidence that their complex digital system can handle rapid transformation without breaking apart.

They will need to ask themselves vital questions and have the competencies to understand the answers:

Can our current information architecture handle larger volumes of data and new data types? What emerging technologies will need to be onboarded to fully leverage new markets and new opportunities? What are the cybersecurity ramifications of new tools, markets, new data, new privacy horizons? How should our organization adapt its risk communications to ensure everyone is onboard and aligned with the new targets? Can we keep the IT and cybersecurity operations teams together, and what help will they need? What's on the regulatory horizon, and how can we get ahead of it? Does our board have the competencies to understand and oversee this level of change?

Thinking like a systems thinker will help leaders safely navigate the storm and find their path forward.

Stage 3 — Catch the Boat

Staying in stagnant red waters isn't ever a winning strategy.

New market opportunities are transforming industries and companies. Look far beyond your usual horizon for signs of blue waters. Speed and innovation will be critical success drivers, allowing those agile enough to capitalize on opportunities as they emerge, or before they do.

How Systems Thinkers Lead

High-reliability organizations, like nuclear power plants, adopt several key cultural qualities intrinsic to how they function at every organizational level.

Systems thinking isn't just for leaders; every employee is a part of the modern organization's complex and dynamic system. Systems thinking and leadership starts in the boardroom and with the CEO but needs to permeate the entire organization.

Here are the cultural traits that leading companies make core to their business at every level:

They create a collective mindfulness — They talk and act like cybersecurity is everyone's responsibility. They reinforce that everyone has a role to play in understanding market shifts and changes and in innovating for the business to respond to them. They reinforce the value they can create by working together, as a well-oiled complex system.

They are preoccupied with failure — They know their systems can fail—catastrophically. They know that the human element is often the weak link. But they also know the human element can frequently be the part stopping the system from failing. They focus on details but understand the big picture and how the details work together to safely deliver value.

They are reluctant to oversimplify — They are not superficial in their analysis or understanding. They know that in a dynamic complex world, there's enormous value in the details. Oversimplification can often be seen in the boardroom by overreliance on scores in understanding cybersecurity risk. They don't view IT as a singular domain but recognize that eight very complex subsystems (DiRECTOR™) need to work together to safely deliver a digital value proposition. They sweat the details on understanding how external forces will flow and impact markets and their business.

They understand the influence of real-time operations — The last mile and last minute have been bridged with the level of digital connectivity we have today. Capitalizing on these dimensions creates unique value propositions but also significant risks. They pay attention and understand the importance of real-time spatial and temporal dynamics throughout their business, and how this influences the external forces impacting them. They operate in a controlled manner but with a sense of urgency. They are calm under fire because they have a deep understanding of the situation and their business system, they are not controlled by it.

They defer to expertise — They welcome and search out experts who can validate and stretch their thinking throughout their business. They know there's extraordinary value in depth of understanding in a complex world and that superficial analysis can often lead to missed opportunities and big mistakes.

They have a top-to-bottom commitment to resilience — Recovering from difficulties, toughness and springing back into shape have never been more valuable traits for any business. Failures will continue to occur, even for systems thinkers and leaders. But the organizations delivering on this key trait post-pandemic will be the ones writing the new rules of the game far into the future.

Summary

The goal with THE GREAT REBOOT is to help leaders develop new patterns of thinking around the complex world, to help them:

1. Understand what a complex system is and know how to identify systemic risk.

2.   Recognize their digital business system as a vital complex system and understand its risks.

3.   Know that COVID-19-influenced systemic change offers extraordinary opportunity which can leverage the same patterns of systems thinking.

The long-term path to business value creation is the digital one; that is inevitable. New digital tools and technologies will enable new systems and strengthen old ones in new ways. These systems and their changes will continue serving the global population's diverse needs and wants and our systems are guaranteed to remain complex in delivering on these many needs.

We have two choices: to ignore their complexity and take our chances; or to reboot and understand them and make them better.

We can also no longer be the weak link in the natural systems occupying our world. They're a part of all of our humanmade systems and we need to help them, help us.

The systems thinkers and leaders who understand these changes along with their opportunities and risks, will be the ones safely navigating the future they're creating.

And what a magnificent future it can be.

Or, we do nothing. And take our chances...

Acknowledgements

In preparing this book, we received inspiration and support from many business leaders who worked alongside us with a common aim: to advance the practice and profession of digital and cybersecurity risk oversight in America's boardrooms and beyond.

These leaders see the realm of the possible in a more effective approach to how we design, build and secure our digital future.

We'd like to recognize the members of Digital Directors Network (www.digitaldirectors.network) and especially those CIOs, CISOs, corporate directors and other technology leaders who have acquired their certification as board-Qualified Technology Experts (QTEs). Digital success starts with their boardroom leadership.

A special thank you on this journey to Jerry Nowicki, Andrew Chrostowski, John Hotta, Kazu Yozawa, Jeff Anderson, Professor Joe Tranquillo, Bob Kress, Kelly Bissell, Sherri Douville, Maryfran Johnson, Michael Piacente and Paul Bergman.

Endnotes

[1] What's Next: 200 CEOs look into the future of business. Business Insider, May 12, 2020: https://www.businessinsider.com/what-is-next-ceos-future-business-leaders-covid-19-2020-5

[2] Ibid

[3] 3 restaurateurs on how the beleaguered food-service industry is weathering the coronavirus pandemic: https://fortune.com/2020/04/20/coroanvirus-restaurants-food-service-industry-takeout-delivery-covid-19/

[4] Trying to Picture Life for Restaurants after COVID-19: https://www.qsrmagazine.com/fast-food/trying-picture-life-restaurants-after-covid-19

[5] The Economic Impact of the Meat Industry in the U.S.: https://www.meatinstitute.org/index.php?ht=a/GetDocument Action/i/93337

[6] www.beyondmeat.com

[7] The Non-Paranoid Person's Guide to Viruses Escaping From Labs: https://www.motherjones.com/politics/2020/05/the-non-paranoid-persons-guide-to-viruses-escaping-from-labs/

[8] Wendy's asks 'where's the beef?": https://www.linkedin.com/feed/news/wendys-asks-wheres-the-beef-4835916/

[9] What's Next: 200 CEOs look into the future of business. Business Insider, May 12, 2020:

https://www.businessinsider.com/what-is-next-ceos-future-business-leaders-covid-19-2020-5

[10] Root Cause Analysis -Challenger Explosion: https://www.thinkreliability.com/case_studies/root-cause-analysis-challenger-explosion/

[11] Challenger Cost: $3.2 Billion: https://www.latimes.com/archives/la-xpm-1986-03-11-mn-3099-story.html

[12] 2019, "Internet-Organized Crime Threat Assessment," European Union Agency for Law Enforcement Cooperation (EUROPOL) https://www.europol.europa.eu/iocta-report

[13] Ransomware Demands: $170B Worldwide Forecast in 2020 Report: https://www.msspalert.com/cybersecurity-breaches-and-attacks/ransomware/demand-costs-2020-research/

[14] 15% of Ransomware Victims Paid Ransom in 2019: https://www.darkreading.com/edge/theedge/15--of-ransomware-victims-paid-ransom-in-2019-quadrupling-2018-/b/d-id/1335147?image_number=1

[15] Must-Know Ransomware Statistics and Attack Trends for 2020: https://www.ninjarmm.com/blog/must-know-ransomware-statistics-2020/

[16] Airbnb's Enhanced Cleaning Initiative for the Future of Travel: https://news.airbnb.com/en-us/airbnbs-enhanced-cleaning-initiative-for-the-future-of-travel/

[17] PG&E settles wildfire claims with insurers for $11 billion: https://www.reuters.com/article/us-pg-e-corp-wildfire-claims/pge-reaches-11-billion-settlement-relating-to-wildfire-claims-idUSKCN1VY1FN

[18] What's Next: 200 CEOs look into the future of business. Business Insider, May 12, 2020: https://www.businessinsider.com/what-is-next-ceos-future-business-leaders-covid-19-2020-5

[19] Action, James and Hibbs, Mark, March 2012. "Why Fukushima Was Preventable," The Carnegie Papers, Carnegie Endowment for International Peace.

[20] Acton, James and Hibbs, Mark, 2012. "Why Fukushima Was Preventable," Carnegie Endowment For International Peace, Washington, D.C.

[21] What's Next: 200 CEOs look into the future of business. Business Insider, May 12, 2020: https://www.businessinsider.com/what-is-next-ceos-future-business-leaders-covid-19-2020-5

[22] Jamison, D. T., H. Gelband, S. Horton, P. Jha, R. Laxminarayan, C. N. Mock, and R. Nugent, editors. 2018. Disease Control Priorities: Improving Health and Reducing Poverty. Disease Control Priorities (third edition), Volume 9. Washington, DC: World Bank. doi:10.1596/978-1-4648-0527-1. License: Creative Commons Attribution CC BY 3.0 IGO

[23] 2020 edition AHA Hospital Statistics: https://www.aha.org/system/files/media/file/2020/01/2020-aha-hospital-fast-facts-new-Jan-2020.pdf

149

[24] CDC website data gathered on April 21st 2020: www.cdc.gov

[25] U.S. Health Care from a Global Perspective, 2019: Higher Spending, Worse Outcomes: https://www.commonwealthfund.org/sites/default/files/2020-01/Tikkanen_US_hlt_care_global_perspective_2019_OECD_db_v2.pdf

[26] Bush, George W., November 1, 2005, National Institutes of Health speech. Bethesda, MD. https://georgewbush-whitehouse.archives.gov/news/releases/2005/11/20051101-1.html

[27] Shaping the Future of Digital Economy and New Value Creation: https://www.weforum.org/platforms/shaping-the-future-of-digital-economy-and-new-value-creation

[28] Source IDC private email on May 5th, 2020, www.idc.com

[29] OpsRamps, Thriving in the New Normal, April 2020 https://info.opsramp.com/IT-spending-new-normal

[30] Tranquillo, Joe (2019). An Introduction to Complex Systems – Making Sense of a Changing World, Springer Nature

[31] What's Next: 200 CEOs look into the future of business. Business Insider, May 12, 2020: https://www.businessinsider.com/what-is-next-ceos-future-business-leaders-covid-19-2020-5

[32] COSO Enterprise Risk Management – Integrated Framework, 2004, COSO: https://www.coso.org/Pages/erm.aspx

[33] COSO Enterprise Risk Management – Integrating with Strategy and Performance, p. 10, COSO, 2017: https://www.coso.org/Pages/erm.aspx

[34] What Table Games Have the Best (And Worst) Odds in Vegas?: https://www.casino.org/blog/vegas-casinos-games-odds/

[35] Payne, Graeme. (2020). The New Era of Cybersecurity Breaches, Cumming, GA. Cybersecurity Executive Advisors LLC.

[36] Ibid

[37] Equifax Settles Mega-Breach Lawsuit for $1.38 Billion: https://www.bankinfosecurity.com/equifaxs-class-action-done-dusted-a-13608

[38] The Evil Internet Minute 2019: https://www.riskiq.com/infographic/evil-internet-minute-2019/

[39]The 2020 Official Annual Cybercrime Report: https://www.herjavecgroup.com/the-2019-official-annual-cybercrime-report/

[40] Cybercriminals raking in $1.5 trillion every year: https://www.techrepublic.com/article/cybercriminals-raking-in-1-5-trillion-every-year/

[41] Appendix D: Fundamentals of the Funds Transfer Process: https://www.fincen.gov/sites/default/files/shared/Appendix_D.pdf

[42] Office of Financial Research 2016 Financial Stability Report: https://www.financialresearch.gov/financial-stability-reports/files/OFR_2016_Financial-Stability-Report.pdf

[43] Ibid.

[44] OpsRamp, 2019. Thriving In The New Normal https://info.opsramp.com/IT-spending-new-normal

[45] When Zoom was young: the early years: https://vator.tv/news/2020-03-26-when-zoom-was-young-the-early-years

[46] Meet Zoom billionaire Eric Yuan, who's made $4 billion in 2020 so far - Business Insider: https://www.businessinsider.com/meet-zoom-billionaire-eric-yuan-career-net-worth-life

[47] When Zoom was young: the early years: https://vator.tv/news/2020-03-26-when-zoom-was-young-the-early-years

[48] Zoom grows to 3000 million meeting participants despite the security backlash: https://www.theverge.com/2020/4/23/21232401/zoom-300-million-users-growth-coronavirus-pandemic-security-privacy-concerns-response

[49] Zoom and Google Hangouts Banned by large companies and government organizations: https://www.businessinsider.in/tech/news/companies-and-organisations-that-have-banned-zoom-and-google-hangouts/articleshow/75156719.cms

[50] Zoom's daily active users jumped from 10 million to over 200 million in 3 months | VentureBeat: https://venturebeat.com/2020/04/02/zooms-daily-active-users-jumped-from-10-million-to-over-200-million-in-3-months/

[51] Zoom Hits Milestone on 90-Day Security Plan, Releases Zoom 5.0: https://blog.zoom.us/wordpress/2020/04/22/zoom-hits-milestone-on-90-day-security-plan-releases-zoom-5-0/

[52] 90-Day Security Plan Progress Report: April 22: https://zoom.us/docs/doc/Ask-Eric-Anything-422.pdf

[53] FTC Imposes $5 Billion Penalty and Sweeping New Privacy Restrictions on Facebook: https://www.ftc.gov/news-events/press-releases/2019/07/ftc-imposes-5-billion-penalty-sweeping-new-privacy-restrictions

[54] 2018-2019 NACD Public Company Governance Survey, NACD, Arlington, VA

[55] What's Next: 200 CEOs look into the future of business. Business Insider, May 12, 2020: https://www.businessinsider.com/what-is-next-ceos-future-business-leaders-covid-19-2020-5

Made in the USA
Columbia, SC
12 June 2020